The Options Course Workbook

Founded in 1807, John Wiley & Sons is the oldest independent publishing company in the United States. With offices in North America, Europe, Australia, and Asia, Wiley is globally committed to developing and marketing print and electronic products and services for our customers' professional and personal knowledge and understanding.

The Wiley Trading series features books by traders who have survived the market's ever changing temperament and have prospered—some by reinventing systems, others by getting back to basics. Whether a novice trader, professional, or somewhere in-between, these books will provide the advice and strategies needed to prosper today and well into the future.

For a list of available titles, visit our web site at www.WileyFinance.com.

The Options Course Workbook

Second Edition

***Step-by-Step Exercises and Tests to Help You Master* The Options Course**

GEORGE A. FONTANILLS

John Wiley & Sons, Inc.

Published by John Wiley & Sons, Inc., Hoboken, New Jersey.
Published simultaneously in Canada.

For general information on our other products and services, or technical support, please contact our Customer Care Department within the United States at 800-762-2974, outside the United States at 317-572-3993 or fax 317-572-4002.

Wiley also publishes its books in a variety of electronic formats. Some content that appears in print may not be available in electronic books.

For more information about Wiley products, visit our web site at www.wiley.com.

ISBN 0-471-69421-5

Printed in the United States of America.

10 9 8 7 6 5 4 3 2 1

To our global community
that we may strive to create
a peaceful world
for all our children.

Contents

The Options Course Workbook

CHAPTER 1

Options Trading: A Primer

SUMMARY

Starting to trade options can be stressful and unsettling, but it doesn't have to be. By learning to trade options systematically and by fostering a patient approach, a new trader can become successful. Options trading requires an understanding of the characteristics of options and this takes time to master. Nonetheless, a person who is willing to study and work hard can achieve success.

To become successful at trading options, you need to focus on three important features of options: duration, direction, and magnitude. If understood, the interrelation of these three issues can provide the edge needed to win at options trading. There are, however, some steppingstones that need to be put in place before jumping headlong into the options game. Following the suggestions in this book will enable you to gain the knowledge and skills necessary to trade profitably. Mainly, a new trader should start small, not placing too much capital in any one trade initially. New traders should also paper trade strategies to get a better feel for how each strategy works. Any trader, new or experienced, should define the risk before entering any trade. Only consistent risk managers make it in the trading profession; so do your homework and follow the steps outlined in this book.

QUESTIONS AND EXERCISES

1. True or False: Just because someone is licensed to place a trade does not mean the person has the knowledge to invest your money wisely.

2. What is the difference between an investor and a trader?

   ____

   ____

   ____

3. Successful options traders use only ______________ that are readily available and can be invested in a sound manner.
   A. Options.
   B. Funds.
   C. Futures.
   D. Stocks.

4. It is critical to accurately assess your ______________ to determine the style of investing that suits you best.
   A. Flexibility.
   B. Interest.
   C. Markets.
   D. Time constraints.

5. How can you minimize your losses when you first begin trading options?
   A. Start small.
   B. Learn to paper trade.
   C. Interview several brokers before picking the one most suited to your needs.
   D. All of the above.

6. What is the most important factor for building a low-stress investment strategy?
   A. Understanding your markets.
   B. Having a good broker.
   C. Defining your risk in every trade.
   D. Learning to paper trade first.

7. ______________ allows a trader to cultivate a matrix of strategies with which to respond to market movement in any direction.
   A. Flexibility.
   B. Specializing.
   C. Computer access.
   D. Confidence.

8. Successful investors usually ______________ in just one or in a few areas. This allows them to develop strategies that work in certain recognizable market conditions.
   A. Specialize.
   B. Win.
   C. Go short.
   D. Systematically invest.

9. To become a successful options trader you have to have ______________.
   A. Lots of money to invest.
   B. Patience and persistence.
   C. A computer.
   D. A good sense of market direction.

MEDIA ASSIGNMENT

The Internet is a great resource for new and experienced traders. Not only can traders place trades online, but there is a plethora of free options information that can be easily accessed. For example, the Optionetics web site has a wide range of information and numerous articles that can foster profitable trading for both new and experienced traders. Take the time to become familiar with the Optionetics site in order to benefit from the tools and information found there. This is also a great starting point to find a broker. The site offers a section dedicated to providing in-depth information about the various options brokers out there. Take the time to review this information so you'll be prepared to open a brokerage account when the time comes.

VOCABULARY LIST

Bear
Broker
Bull
Call
Capital
Delta neutral
Go long
Go short
Investor
Leverage
Paper trading
Put
Return
Risk
Risk management
Stop loss
Trader

SOLUTIONS

1. True or False: Just because someone is licensed to place a trade does not mean the person has the knowledge to invest your money wisely.

   Answer: True.

   Discussion: Unfortunately, obtaining a license to place a trade does not necessarily make someone a good trader. Like many things in life, sometimes book knowledge isn't enough to create success. When learning to drive a car, someone doesn't just immediately move out onto the freeway after reading a book. Though having a license does teach some important things, it isn't a guarantee that the person will be successful at trading.

2. What is the difference between an investor and a trader?

   Answer: An investor takes a long-term, passive approach. A trader takes a more active approach using various options strategies that tend to capitalize on shorter-term market movement.

   Discussion: As the term implies, an investor is investing his/her money into a company by buying stock in it. A trader isn't necessarily concerned with ownership, just profits and short-term gains. Most investors are people who buy and hold stock or mutual funds; they are more in step with the Warren Buffett approach to long-term security. A trader seeks profits in the short term, trading stocks and options with a clear eye on risk management and a friendly ear for volatility. Undoubtedly there are many who dabble somewhere in between.

3. Successful options traders use only ____________ that are readily available and can be invested in a sound manner.

   Answer: B—Funds.

   Discussion: Though Optionetics teaches traders how to use options to limit risk, there still is a chance that the capital used in trading options could all be lost. As a result, it is wise to only use money that is not needed for bills or other important necessities in life. If you trade using capital you cannot afford to lose, it is very difficult to trade without letting your emotions get in the way.

4. It is critical to accurately assess your ____________ to determine the style of investing that suits you best.

   Answer: D—Time constraints.

   Discussion: If the capital you plan on using to trade options is also needed for an important life event in the next year or two, it is unwise to use it. Though quick profits can often be made trading options, we still need to trade with a long-term goal in mind. Even a successful options trader might go through a losing streak, and if the capital is needed during this down time, it can be a difficult situation.

5. How can you minimize your losses when you first begin trading options?

   Answer: D—All of the above (start small, learn to paper trade, interview several brokers before picking the one most suited to your needs).

   Discussion: All of these issues should be used when first starting to trade options. The nice thing about options is that it doesn't take a huge amount of capital to get started. Nonetheless, even if you have a nice nest egg to begin with, start small. Try to learn how the strategies work before taking a bigger leap. You may want to paper trade a new strategy so you won't lose capital during the learning process. Even so, there eventually comes a time when the trader will not be able to learn more until he or she trades with real capital. Using a broker who gets a trade a good fill and is easy to work with is crucial for the long-term success of an options trader. With the number of brokers available, don't be afraid to change brokers if the one you start with isn't working out.

6. What is the most important factor for building a low-stress investment strategy?

   Answer: C—Defining your risk in every trade.

   Discussion: Those who pay attention to Optionetics instructors and writers will hear this all the time. Options were first developed to help traders limit risk, and Optionetics still believes this is the key. We need to know the risk of every trade before we enter it so that we are prepared for the worst and know what actions are needed to limit this risk.

7. _____________ allows a trader to cultivate a matrix of strategies with which to respond to market movement in any direction.

   Answer: A—Flexibility.

   Discussion: Though it is a good idea to narrow your choice of strategies, this doesn't mean that a trader shouldn't have a couple of strategies for each type of market. One of the greatest advantages to trading options is their flexibility. You can make money in up, down, and sideways markets using options, so don't limit yourself to just bullish strategies.

8. Successful investors usually _____________ in just one or in a few areas. This allows them to develop strategies that work in certain recognizable market conditions.

   Answer: A—Specialize.

   Discussion: Specialization has become the thing to do in any profession in our day and age. It is no different when trading options. Though we need to have a wide base of knowledge about options and trading, we do not need to become experts in every available options strategy. As you learn about different options strategies, specialize in the ones that best fit your risk tolerance and expertise.

9. To become a successful options trader you have to have _____________.

   Answer: B—Patience and persistence.

   Discussion: This is very important to remember. Too many new traders expect to become millionaires overnight; this is unrealistic. Traders need to realize that where there is more possible reward, there is usually a higher degree of risk. Even the most successful options traders often lose money in individual trades. However, these traders have learned to limit their risk and have developed a sound plan that allows them to be patient and persistent.

MEDIA ASSIGNMENT

Learning to use the Internet to further your understanding of the market and options is a vital part of your trading education. The free Optionetics web site has a plethora of information. Mainly, take the time to search for information dealing with the initial strategies you want to master. As you progress up the learning curve, read the daily articles to gain an understanding of the markets. You can also read about various options brokers on the Brokers Review link. This will provide information about costs, services, and other important data about most of the options brokers available.

VOCABULARY DEFINITIONS

Bear: An investor who believes that a security or the market is falling or is expected to fall.

Broker: An individual or firm that charges a fee or commission for executing buy and sell orders submitted by another individual or firm.

Bull: An investor who believes that a security or the market is rising or is expected to rise.

Call: An option contract that gives the holder the right, but not the obligation, to buy a specified amount of an underlying security at a specified price within a specified time (e.g., if you buy an IBM January 85 call, you have the right to buy 100 shares of IBM at $85 each by the third Friday in January).

Capital: The amount of money you have invested. When your investing objective is capital preservation, your priority is to try not to lose any money. When your objective is capital growth, your priority is to try to make your initial investment grow in value. Capital also refers to accumulated money or goods available for use in producing more money or goods.

Delta neutral: Refers to an options position constructed so that the profitability of the position relies on the magnitude of the move—not the directional bias; it is relatively insensitive to the price movement of the underlying instruments. A delta neutral trade is arranged by selecting a calculated ratio of short and long positions with a combined delta of zero.

Go long: To buy securities, options, or futures with the intent to profit from a rise in the price of the assets.

Go short: To sell securities, options, or futures with the intent to profit from a drop in the price of the assets.

Investor: A person whose principal concern in the purchase of a security is the minimizing of long-term risk, compared to the speculator who is prepared to accept calculated risk in the hope of making better-than-average profits, or the gambler who is prepared to take even greater risks. More generally, it refers to people who invest money in investment products.

Leverage: Enables a trader to buy or sell a security or derivative and receive fair value for it using borrowed capital to increase investment return.

Paper trading: Simulating a trade without actually putting up the money, usually done for the purpose of gaining additional trading experience.

Put: An option contract that gives the owner the right, but not the obligation, to sell a specified amount of an underlying security at a specified price within a specified time.

Return: The income earned or a capital gain made on an investment.

Risk: The potential financial loss inherent in an investment.

Risk management: The process of managing trades by hedging risk.

Stop-loss order: An order to sell when the price of the stock declines to, or below, a stated price. The purpose of this is to reduce the amount of loss that might occur.

Trader: Someone who buys and sells frequently with the objective of short-term profit.

CHAPTER 2

The Big Picture

SUMMARY

Trading stocks might be the best-known form of playing the markets, but many individuals specialize in other lesser-known trading instruments. This chapter is designed to give the novice trader a comprehensive view of trading by exploring the wide variety of different trading instruments—including stocks, futures, and options—as well as the multitude of ways to trade them. Particular attention is devoted to trading instrument properties as well as specific examples.

Options are derivatives, meaning they derive their value from an underlying financial instrument. Though options can be entered using stock as the underlying security, indexes and futures also have options available. Futures and options can be used together, but they are two distinctly different instruments and require totally different types of trading accounts. However, both of these instruments provide increased leverage, which means a trader can control a large amount of stock or other instrument with little initial capital outlay.

Options are an extremely versatile instrument and can be used to create a variety of different limited risk strategies. However, like most endeavors, they require practice and discipline, as well as proper money and risk management. In addition, traders must pay significant attention to volatility issues if options are to be successfully utilized. Both historical and implied volatility are important concepts to understand and should be studied in depth to master the options trading game.

QUESTIONS AND EXERCISES

1. A stock is a unit of ownership in a company. The value of that unit of ownership is based on a number of factors, including:

   ____

   ____

2. Six people form a company together and decide that there will be only six shareholders with only one share each. If this company's assets total $90,000 and it has $15,000 in liabilities, how much is each share worth?

   A. $15,000.

   B. $12,500.

   C. $10,000.

   D. $7,500.

3. The computerized market, ______________, is also referred to as the over-the-counter (OTC) market.

   A. Securities and Exchange Commission.

   B. Chicago Board Options Exchange.

   C. Nasdaq.

   D. FOREX.

4. Supply and demand for a company's shares helps to create ______________.

   A. Momentum.

   B. Historical volatility.

   C. Liquidity.

   D. Time decay.

5. If investors feel a company will beat Wall Street expectations, then the price of the shares will be ______________ as there will be more buyers than sellers.

   A. Higher.

   B. Lower.

   C. Bid up.

   D. Offer down.

6. If the majority of investors feel that the company's earnings will disappoint the Street, then the prices will be _____________.
   A. Higher.
   B. Lower.
   C. Bid up.
   D. Offer down.

7. If there are more bidders (buyers), prices will _____________. If there are more people offering (sellers), prices will _____________.
   A. Fall. Rise.
   B. Rise. Fall.
   C. Stay the same.
   D. Be impossible to predict.

8. A company's board of directors decides whether to declare _____________ from time to time to be paid out and distributed to shareholders on a payable date.
   A. Better than expected earnings.
   B. Revised expected earnings.
   C. Cash flow.
   D. A dividend.

9. What are the four unofficial size classifications of stocks?
   1. ____
   2. ____
   3. ____
   4. ____

10. The _____________, which reports the performance of 30 major companies representing key industries, is the most widely quoted indicator of market performance.
    A. Standard & Poor's Index.
    B. Amex Market Value Index.
    C. New York Stock Exchange Composite Index.
    D. Dow Jones Industrial Average.

11. Name a few stock sectors.

____

____

12. What is the difference between a futures contract and an options contract?

____

____

13. _____________ were initially used by farmers and producers of products to hedge themselves or lock in prices for a certain crop or product cycle.
    A. Options contracts.
    B. Futures contracts.
    C. Stock contracts.
    D. All of the above.

14. True or False: Hedgers use futures trading to lock in prices and protect themselves from market movement because they are primarily interested in actually receiving or selling the commodities themselves.

15. _____________ do not expect to take delivery of a product; they are in the futures market to try to make money on the price movement of a futures contract.
    A. Producers.
    B. Speculators.
    C. Hedgers.
    D. Farmers.

16. If you believe soybean prices will rise over the next three months, based on whatever information you may have, you could _________ the corn futures three months out hoping to make a profit.
    A. Go long.
    B. Go short.
    C. Hedge.
    D. All of the above.

17. If you believe corn prices will fall during this same period, you could ______________ the corn futures contract three months out hoping to make a profit.
    A. Go long.
    B. Go short.
    C. Hedge.
    D. All of the above.

18. Physical commodities are any bulk good traded on an exchange or in the cash market; examples include grains, meats, metals, and energies. ________________ include debt instruments (such as bonds), currencies, and indexes.
    A. Index futures.
    B. ETFs.
    C. Financial commodities.
    D. HOLDRS.

19. The value of ______________ primarily depends on interest rates.
    A. Bonds.
    B. Debt instruments.
    C. Eurodollars.
    D. All of the above.

20. Typically, there is an inverse relationship between ______________ and most foreign currencies.
    A. The U.S. dollar.
    B. Interest rates.
    C. Bonds.
    D. All of the above.

21. A/an ______________ is an indicator that is used to measure and report value changes in a specific group of stocks, commodities, or different sectors of the marketplace.
    A. Bond.
    B. Moving average.
    C. Index.
    D. All of the above.

22. By combining futures with ____________, you can create trades in which you limit your risk and maximize your potential profits.
    A. Options.
    B. HOLDRS.
    C. Futures contracts.
    D. All of the above.

23. ____________ are contracts between two parties that convey to the buyer a right, but not an obligation, to buy or sell a specific commodity or stock at a specific price within a specific time period for a premium.
    A. Stocks.
    B. Futures.
    C. Options.
    D. All of the above.

24. The price of an option is referred to as the ____________.
    A. Premium.
    B. Strike price.
    C. Bid-ask price.
    D. Price-earnings (P/E) ratio.

25. The ____________ is defined as the price at which the stock or commodity underlying a call or put option can be purchased or sold over the specified period.
    A. Premium.
    B. Strike price.
    C. Bid-ask price.
    D. Price-earnings (P/E) ratio.

26. An option is no longer valid after its ____________.
    A. Payable date.
    B. Expiration date.
    C. Exercise date.
    D. Assignment date.

27. True or False: Options are available on all stocks.

28. Each stock option (call or put) represents ______________ shares of a stock.
    A. 50.
    B. 100.
    C. 500.
    D. 1,000.

29. True or False: Each futures contract has a set of unique specifications.

30. You must be cautious trading indexes, for a few of them do not have much ______________.
    A. Diversification.
    B. Liquidity.
    C. Cash value.
    D. Flexibility.

31. The most important factors for determining opportunity in a market are ______________.
    A. Volume and cash flow.
    B. Volatility and cash flow.
    C. Liquidity and cash flow.
    D. Liquidity and volatility.

32. ______________ gives you the opportunity to move in and out of a market with ease.
    A. Volatility.
    B. Flexibility.
    C. An inexpensive option.
    D. Liquidity.

33. ______________ measures the amount by which an underlying is expected to fluctuate in a given period of time.
    A. Volatility.
    B. Delta.
    C. Theta.
    D. Liquidity.

MEDIA ASSIGNMENT

There are numerous indexes and ETFs available for the options trader. This chapter provided examples of many of these securities, as well as an introductory discussion of volatility. Take the time to look at daily and weekly price charts of various indexes and ETFs as well as their respective volatility levels. When we look at past movement, we are seeing historical volatility. However, by looking at a chart, we can also become pretty good judges of what type of volatility is going to occur in the future. Use a charting program or the Optionetics web site to eyeball these indexes and ETFs to see which are the most and least volatile. Learning how to view charts and access the plethora of information that is available takes time, so start by viewing the list of ETFs and indexes listed in this chapter of the main book.

VOCABULARY LIST

Assets
Assignment
Bond
Capital gain
Commodity
Dividend
Exchange-traded fund (ETF)
Exercise
Futures
Hedgers
Historic volatility
Implied volatility
Liability
Liquidity
Option premium
Payable date
Speculator
Stock
Strike price

SOLUTIONS

1. A stock is a unit of ownership in a company. The value of that unit of ownership is based on a number of factors, including:

   Answer: The total number of outstanding shares; the value of the equity of the company (what it owns less what it owes); the earnings the company produces now and is expected to produce in the future; and the demand for the shares of the company.

Discussion: Stock ownership is a way to participate in the growth of a company. It has limited liability, yet many millionaires have been created by their stock ownership. Fundamental analysis can help buy-and-hold investors find appropriate long-term stocks to own. However, short-term traders normally focus more on technical indicators that include price and volume and supply and demand issues.

2. Six people form a company together and decide that there will be only six shareholders with only one share each. If this company's assets total $90,000 and it has $15,000 in liabilities, how much is each share worth?

   Answer: B—$12,500.

   Discussion: Because the balance sheet says the company is worth $75,000, each one of the six shares would be worth $12,500 ($75,000 ÷ 6 = $12,500). This is called book value, but book value is rarely what a stock trades for in the stock market. Traders are buying future earnings, and this demand normally increases the stock price well above its book value.

3. The computerized market, ______________, is also referred to as the over-the-counter (OTC) market.

   Answer: C—Nasdaq.

   Discussion: The Nasdaq is a computerized marketplace, with buyers and sellers brought together through a computer system. Supporters of the Nasdaq believe this is a much more efficient way to exchange the buying and selling of shares. Whether this is true or not, the Nasdaq trades more volume on a daily basis than the New York Stock Exchange (NYSE). The Nasdaq is best-known for being a tech-laden index. This is because smaller technology companies have been able to get listed on the Nasdaq more easily than on the NYSE.

4. Supply and demand for a company's shares helps to create ______________.

   Answer: C—Liquidity.

   Discussion: Liquidity is important in the options market, as it helps lessen the spread between the bid and ask prices. It would be impossible to sell an option that is being held if there weren't someone to buy it from you. Market makers are there to help alleviate this problem, but illiquid stocks and options are still difficult to trade and are best left alone. In general, we don't want to mess with stocks that have a volume of less than 300,000 shares a day.

5. If investors feel a company will beat Wall Street expectations, then the price of the shares will be ______________ as there will be more buyers than sellers.

   Answer: C—Bid up.

   Discussion: The basic economic rule of supply and demand is used daily in the stock market. When there is an abundance of buyers, this pushes the price higher until the stock price finds an equilibrium point. When there are more sellers than buyers, the stock price will fall until equilibrium is found to the downside. This is the definition of the free market system and has worked well for centuries. The stock market is a great discounter of news, which means expectations drive stock prices. Once an event takes place, the stock trades on what the expectations were more than the actual results.

6. If the majority of investors feel that the company's earnings will disappoint the Street, then the prices will be ______________.

   Answer: D—Offer down.

   Discussion: Sometimes a stock will gain ground when announced earnings are not good. This happens because expectations were even worse than the actual news. When a stock disappoints, though, it tends to see its stock price offered down as traders jump in to sell on the negative announcement. Sometimes a stock will announce fantastic earnings, but expectations were even higher, so the stock still sees a decline after the announcement.

7. If there are more bidders (buyers), prices will ______________. If there are more people offering (sellers), prices will ______________.

   Answer: B—Rise. Fall.

   Discussion: The price of an investment will react to the forces of supply and demand. If there are more buyers than sellers within the market, and demand is strong, prices move higher. However, when investors are selling and supply is rising, prices tend to fall.

8. A company's board of directors decides whether to declare ______________ from time to time to be paid out and distributed to shareholders on a payable date.

   Answer: D—A dividend.

Discussion: A dividend is a part of a company's profit that is passed on to the shareholders. When companies pay part of their profits to shareholders, those profits are called dividends. This amount is announced before it is paid and is distributed to shareholders of record on a per share basis. The board of directors must declare all dividends. Growth companies usually do not offer dividends, as the board of directors feels the capital is best put to work by investing it back into the company. Utility stocks and other slow moving stocks tend to offer the highest dividends. The dividend yield is figured by taking the amount of the dividend on an annualized basis and dividing it by the stock price.

9. What are the four unofficial size classifications of stocks?

   Answer: Large caps (blue chips), mid-caps, small caps, and micro-caps.

   Discussion: Large-cap stocks represent companies with a capitalization of more than $5 billion. Also commonly referred to as blue chips, large caps are generally mature companies that are regarded as safe investments. They are traded on the major exchanges and provide regular dividends to shareholders—perhaps their most appealing advantage. Mid-cap companies have a market capitalization of between $500 million and $5 billion. Mid-caps typically experience slower growth than small caps and faster growth than large caps. Small caps have a market capitalization of between $150 million and $500 million. They offer traders the opportunity for fast growth and are usually much cheaper than mid-caps or blue-chip stocks. Lower prices give them the ability to generate dramatic price gains. Micro-cap stocks have a market capitalization of less than $150 million. They can be extremely risky investments because a significant percentage of companies fail early in the development cycle for a variety of reasons including poor management, defective marketing strategy, or customer rejection of goods or services offered. Each of the four stock size classifications comes with a unique set of investing objectives.

10. The ______________, which reports the performance of 30 major companies representing key industries, is the most widely quoted indicator of market performance.

    Answer: D—Dow Jones Industrial Average.

    Discussion: The Dow Jones Industrial Average (DJIA or Dow) is still the quintessential barometer of stock market performance and is quoted daily on the evening news. While the DJIA has evolved through the years, the information derived from it is essentially the same. It gauges the stock prices of 30 U.S. companies and reflects developments within the U.S. economy. The Dow is a price-weighted index in that the average prices of all 30 components are added together and one final average is computed. Though not the best representative of the broad stock market, the Dow is the most popular index because it has been around the longest. However, though there are just 30 stocks represented, this index mirrors the broader market on a pretty consistent basis. There are times, though, that the Nasdaq and Dow will diverge, and these are important indicators for technical analysts.

11. Name a few stock sectors.

    Answer: Technologies, defense, retail, health care, financials, consumer products.

    Discussion: There are dozens of different sectors and many subsectors. At times a new sector will be created, like Internet stocks. Analysts track various sectors to get a feel for what stocks are bullish and bearish. Not all sectors move in tandem, and analysts can often find leading indicators for the stock market as a whole by studying individual sectors. There are many exchange-traded funds (ETFs) and indexes that track individual sectors, and many of these are optionable. This allows a trader to choose a direction for an entire sector, rather than just one stock within the group.

12. What is the difference between a futures contract and an options contract?

    Answer: A futures contract is a promise to actually deliver or take delivery of the underlying commodity. In contrast, the purchase of an option provides the right, but not the obligation, to buy (call) or sell (put) the underlying instrument.

    Discussion: Both futures and options can be used to make significant profits. Futures tend to be employed after a trader becomes familiar with options, but not always. Futures often are considered more complicated, but they really aren't; they are just less understood. Many options traders use futures as the underlying instrument for their trades. The purchase of a futures contract comes with the obligation to receive delivery of the commodity, bond, or other instrument by a specific date. The sale of a futures contract comes with the obligation to deliver the commodity, bond, or other financial instrument to the buyer by a certain date. The purchase of an option provides the right, but not an obligation, to buy (in the case of a call) or sell (for a put) the underlying asset.

13. ______________ were initially used by farmers and producers of products to hedge themselves or lock in prices for a certain crop or product cycle.

    Answer: B—Futures contracts.

    Discussion: Individuals or corporations can use futures to get a certain price for a commodity. Farmers use futures to lock in the price of corn or wheat a year in advance, which makes it easier to run their farms. However, the vast majority of futures traders are now speculators who have no interest in making or taking delivery of a product—they are just trying to profit from a directional move in the underlying instrument.

14. True or False: Hedgers use futures trading to lock in prices and protect themselves from market movement because they are primarily interested in actually receiving or selling the commodities themselves.

    Answer: True.

    Discussion: A hedger is an investor who uses the futures market to minimize the risk in his or her business. Hedgers may be manufacturers, portfolio managers, bankers, farmers, or others. For example, an oil company can sell its product with a futures contract before it is actually produced and ready for sale. By purchasing a futures contract, the oil company can lock in the prices of oil at a certain point to guarantee the price it will receive.

15. ______________ do not expect to take delivery of a product; they are in the futures market to try to make money on the price movement of a futures contract.

    Answer: B—Speculators.

    Discussion: Unlike hedgers, speculators are using futures to make profits, not limit their risk. In fact, these two types of futures traders need each other. Hedgers use futures to limit risk, while speculators use risk to make large profits. The two have a symbiotic relationship that is necessary to keep the futures market working.

16. If you believe soybean prices will rise over the next three months, based on whatever information you may have, you could ______________ the corn futures three months out hoping to make a profit.

    Answer: A—Go long.

    Discussion: Futures work just like stocks or call options; we want the underlying to rise when we buy a futures contract. Of course, like the stock market in general, futures will be priced based on the expectations for the commodity. If everyone expects it to be a tough winter, then orange futures might drop in value. However, if you speculate that the winter won't be as bad as expected, you would benefit from buying a future if your belief turns into reality.

17. If you believe corn prices will fall during this same period, you could ______________ the corn futures contract three months out hoping to make a profit.

    Answer: B—Go short.

    Discussion: Going short involves selling a futures contract; this is very risky, akin to shorting stock. However, for experienced traders, shorting a futures contract might make sense. Normally, if we want to participate in the down movement of a commodity or stock, we are best served by buying puts. This strategy limits the position's risk, but still provides ample profit opportunities.

18. Physical commodities are any bulk good traded on an exchange or in the cash market; examples include grains, meats, metals, and energies. ______________ include debt instruments (such as bonds), currencies, and indexes.

    Answer: C—Financial commodities.

    Discussion: Financial commodities have become increasingly popular with options traders. A futures contract of a financial commodity is an obligation to buy or sell a specific quantity of currency or some other financial instrument for a predetermined price by a designated date. Like any futures, those based on financial commodities are mostly used by speculators, though there are some hedgers who use them to hedge other holdings. By using options, traders can hedge the risk that comes with the purchase (or sale) of a financial commodity. Other physical commodities include the raw materials used in most retail and manufactured products. The five major categories are grains, metals, energies, raw foods, and meats. Some are seasonal in nature (heating oil, for instance), which causes demand to fluctuate based on the time of year and climactic conditions. Others react to specific events; a drought in the Midwest can send grain prices soaring. Commodities are also highly leveraged investments. A small amount of cash can control many times its face value in commodities contracts. But this works both ways, creating huge potential wins and losses. Futures are used by farmers and holders to hedge prices in the future, but futures on physical commodities still have plenty of speculators as well. The Chicago Board of Trade (CBOT) is the major exchange for these commodities.

19. The value of ______________ primarily depends on interest rates.

    Answer: D—All of the above (bonds, debt instruments, Eurodollars).

    Discussion: All of these commodities depend on interest rates. For example, when interest rates go up, bond (loan) prices fall. Conversely, when interest rates fall below the interest rate guaranteed on a specific bond, that bond increases in value. Since interest rates can change the value of these instruments drastically, holders of these instruments will hedge their risk by using options and futures on interest rates and individual commodities like bonds or currencies.

20. Typically, there is an inverse relationship between ______________ and most foreign currencies.

    Answer: A—The U.S. dollar.

    Discussion: Money is greatly affected by international rates of exchange. The value of a country's currency fluctuates in relation to values of foreign currencies. An inverse relationship usually exists between the dollar and other currencies. If the dollar falls, foreign currencies may increase in value. For example, if the U.S. dollar is weak in comparison to the yen, the prices of Japanese products imported to the United States will increase. If the dollar is high in comparison to the euro, the prices of American products exported to Europe will rise. An inverse relationship is created because of the large amount of imports and exports that the United States participates in. Currencies are traded by large financial institutions looking for the best rate of exchange. Since a change in the exchange rate can create such a huge variance for multinational firms, many of these corporations use futures to hedge their risk. Of course, those traders who have a strong understanding of foreign currencies can also speculate on future changes in the value of the dollar as opposed to other currencies.

21. A/an ______________ is an indicator that is used to measure and report value changes in a specific group of stocks, commodities, or different sectors of the marketplace.

    Answer: C—Index.

    Discussion: An index is a select group of stocks that measures and reports value changes to the group as a whole. A variety of indexes are tailored to reflect the performance of many different sectors of the marketplace, such as the S&P 500 ($SPX) or the New York Stock Exchange Composite Index ($NYA). While these indexes are used to gauge trends within the stock market, some indexes are designed to measure the price changes of specific industry groups. Indexes have become increasingly popular over the past 20 years, partly due to the increased volume of shares traded on the exchanges and the ease of creating an index with the proliferation of computers. Regardless of why there are so many indexes, their use has become widespread. Most major exchanges have options and futures available on them, allowing a knowledgeable trader plenty of opportunities to hedge risk and make large profits.

22. By combining futures with ______________, you can create trades in which you limit your risk and maximize your potential profits.

    Answer: A—Options.

    Discussion: Options are the perfect trading instrument for leveraging your capital and hedging stocks and futures against risk. They act to protect your investments just as buying insurance would for your car or home. Many of us probably could have done a better job "insuring" our portfolios against losses, but only hindsight is 20/20. To be successful in today's markets, you need to evaluate your current positions to see what you can do to be more successful moving forward.

23. ______________ are contracts between two parties that convey to the buyer a right, but not an obligation, to buy or sell a specific commodity or stock at a specific price within a specific time period for a premium.

    Answer: C—Options.

    Discussion: The key to this definition is that the buyer has the right, *but not the obligation*, to buy or sell the underlying asset by a certain time. This varies from a futures contract where there *is* an obligation. Options are unique and very versatile instruments that can be used to hedge risk and make substantial profits. However, like all professionals, options traders need to learn their craft and use discipline.

24. The price of an option is referred to as the ______________.

    Answer: A—Premium.

    Discussion: This is a fitting name, as the same term is also used for insurance. This makes sense since options are often used as insurance to protect long-term holdings. When buying a call option, we have the right to buy the underlying security at a future date at a specific price. We do not have to use this right, just as we don't always use our insurance policies (i.e., file a claim), but the option is there if we do want to use it.

25. The ______________ is referred to as the price at which the stock or commodity underlying a call or put option can be purchased or sold over the specified period.

    Answer: B—Strike price.

    Discussion: The strike price has a distinct relationship to the price of an option. If the strike price is a long ways away from the current value of the security, the premium will be low. However, if there already is value in the option because it is in-the-money (ITM), the premium will be much higher.

26. An option is no longer valid after its ______________.

    Answer: B—Expiration date.

    Discussion: Once an option hits its expiration date, which is close of business prior to the Saturday following the third Friday of each month, it can no longer be exercised. If an option is out-of-the-money (OTM) at expiration, it will no longer have any value. However, if it is ITM, the option holder will need to either sell it for its current value or exercise the option to fulfill the contract. Most options contracts are bought and sold before expiration.

27. True or False: Options are available on all stocks.

    Answer: False.

    Discussion: Options are not always available on every stock. Options are often added to new stocks, but only about 40 percent of current stocks traded on the major exchanges or optionable. If a stock has little liquidity, there is very little reason to start trading options on the stock. The CBOE web site has a list of new optionable stocks that can be viewed or e-mailed to you each day.

28. Each stock option (call or put) represents ______________ shares of a stock.

    Answer: B—100.

    Discussion: Generally a stock option represents 100 shares of stock. Thus, if a call option is quoted at $2, the total cost for one contract would be $200. If the stock is trading for $20, this means we are controlling $2,000 worth of stock for $200, which is leverage of 10-to-1. This allows options traders to make large profits without an overwhelming amount of risk.

29. True or False: Each futures contract has a set of unique specifications.

    Answer: True.

    Discussion: You are responsible for understanding the specifications for each futures market. Each commodity has different specifications when it comes to futures. This makes sense, as different commodities are measured in different ways. With stock, we have a share; with gold, we measure it by the ounce. Thus, each futures contract can have a different ratio that needs to be calculated to come up with the premium and underlying value.

30. You must be cautious trading indexes, for a few of them do not have much ______________.

    Answer: B—Liquidity.

    Discussion: We need to be cautious not only with indexes that do not have much liquidity, but with any underlying security that is illiquid. A lack of liquidity creates higher bid-ask spreads and also leads to a great deal of volatility. When there is little interest in a security or index, it is more difficult to get a good fill when you are ready to sell.

31. The most important factors for determining opportunity in a market are ______________.

    Answer: D—Liquidity and volatility.

    Discussion: Liquidity is the measure of trading volume of an investment security. As a general rule, the more trading volume associated with an investment, the more liquid, and the better the market. Volatility is a measure of the speed or movement in a market. A very volatile market moves fast and can provide a trader with a greater number of profit-making opportunities.

32. ______________ gives you the opportunity to move in and out of a market with ease.

    Answer: D—Liquidity.

    Discussion: If an option is illiquid it can result in bad fills and wide bid-ask spreads. With stocks, we want to see volume of at least 300,000 shares traded on a daily basis. For options, volume doesn't necessarily have to be large, but there should be open interest of at least 100 contracts. It's easy to distinguish the options and stocks that have low liquidity, as the bid and ask prices will be farther apart.

33. _____________ measures the amount by which an underlying is expected to fluctuate in a given period of time.

Answer: A—Volatility.

Discussion: Volatility is a percentage that measures the amount by which the underlying stock or option is expected to change in a given period of time. A stock's volatility has a significant effect on the price of its options. A highly volatile stock has a better chance of making a substantial move than a low-volatility stock. A more volatile asset offers larger swings upward or downward in price in shorter time spans than less volatile assets. Large movements, in turn, are attractive to options traders who are always looking for big directional swings to make their contracts profitable. Therefore, the options of a high-volatility stock generally command higher premiums. Implied volatility tells a trader how much a stock is expected to move and is a crucial element in the pricing of an option. Understanding implied volatility is one of the most crucial factors in becoming a successful options trader.

MEDIA ASSIGNMENT

With the proliferation of new indexes and ETFs, take the time to view charts of these instruments. Look for volatile issues and get a feel for how these securities move. Then choose a handful of stocks in various sectors and watch them to see how they react and perform. Even if we stick strictly to individual stock options, learning to gauge the entire sector is an important part of choosing the appropriate direction. Looking at the volatility of a sector can also provide us with a better understanding of the volatility of an individual stock within that sector.

VOCABULARY DEFINITIONS

Asset: A balance sheet item expressing what an individual or a corporation owns.

Assignment: Refers to the option writer's (seller's) obligation to sell or buy a stock or other financial instrument at the strike price for which the writer sold the contract. The buyer of an option has the right (but not the obligation) to exercise the option—that is, buy the underlying asset at the strike price of the contract (long call) or sell (deliver) the underlying asset to the option writer at the strike price of the contract (long put). Assignment means the options writer receives an exercise notice by another options writer that requires him to sell (in the case of a call) or purchase (in the case of a put) the underlying security at the specified strike price.

Bond: A debt obligation issued by a government (i.e., Treasury bond) or corporation (i.e., corporate bond) that promises to pay its bondholders periodic interest at a fixed rate (the coupon), and to repay the principal of the loan at maturity (a specified future date). Bonds are usually issued with a par or face value of $1,000, representing the principal or amount of money borrowed. The interest payment is stated on the face of the bond at issue.

Capital gain: The profit realized when a capital asset is sold for a higher price than the purchase price. Your costs (when you buy) include the commission you paid your broker and are deducted from the proceeds when you sell. In a mutual fund, capital gains are created when the fund buys and sells securities. These gains are then distributed to shareholders at least annually. Shareholders can also earn capital gains by redeeming their units at higher prices than they originally paid.

Commodity: Any bulk good traded on an exchange or in the cash market; examples include metals, grains, and meats.

Dividend: When companies pay part of their profits to shareholders, those payments are called dividends. A mutual fund's dividend is money paid to shareholders that comes from the investment income the fund has earned. This amount is announced before it is paid and is distributed to shareholders of record on a per share basis. Dividends may be in the form of cash, stock, or property. The board of directors must declare all dividends.

Exchange-traded fund (ETF): A fund that tracks an index, but can be traded like a stock. Many ETFs have options available allowing traders to profit from moves within a sector.

Exercise: To implement the right of the holder of an option to buy (in the case of a call) or sell (in the case of a put) the underlying security. When you exercise an option, you carry out the terms of an option contract.

Futures: A term used to designate all contracts covering the purchase and sale of financial instruments or physical commodities for future delivery on a commodity futures exchange.

Hedger: A trader who enters the market with the intent to protect a position in the underlying asset; an investor who uses the futures market to minimize the risk in his or her business. Hedgers may be manufacturers, portfolio managers, bankers, farmers, and so on. Hedgers also use options to protect stock positions. For example, an investor can use a put to hedge a stock or an index put to hedge a stock portfolio.

Historic volatility: Calculated by using the standard deviation of underlying asset price changes from close-to-close of trading going back 21 to 23 days. A measurement of how much a contract price has fluctuated over a specific period of time in the past; usually calculated by taking a standard deviation of price changes over a time period.

Implied volatility: The volatility computed using the actual market prices of an option contract and one of a number of pricing models. For example, if the market price of an option rises without a change in the price of the underlying stock or future, implied volatility will have risen.

Liability: A legal obligation to pay a debt owed. Current liabilities are debts payable within 12 months. Long-term liabilities are debts payable over a period of more than 12 months.

Liquidity: The ease with which an asset can be converted to cash in the marketplace. A large number of buyers and sellers and a high volume of trading activity provide high liquidity. Liquidity is a concern for any moneys that may be required on short notice, whether for emergencies or for planned purchases.

Option premium: The price of an option; the amount of money that the option holder pays for the rights and the option writer receives for the obligations granted by the option.

Payable date: The date on which a declared stock dividend or a bond interest payment is scheduled to be paid.

Speculator: An investor or trader who is willing to take large risks for a chance to make large gains. For example, buying a very volatile stock and hoping to sell it a day or a week later at a higher price is speculative trading. Speculators sometimes buy puts and calls in anticipation of a short-term move higher or lower in the underlying asset. In the futures market, a speculator is a trader who hopes to profit from a directional move in the underlying instrument and attempts to anticipate price changes and, through buying and selling futures contracts, aims to make profits. A speculator doesn't use the futures market in connection with the production, processing, marketing, or handling of a product. The speculator has no interest in making or taking delivery.

Stock: A share of a company's stock translates into ownership of part of the company. Thus, when you own any shares of a company's stock, you own part of the company. How much you own depends on how many shares of stock you have. Holders of common stock are the last to be paid any profits from the company but are likely to profit most from any growth it has. Owners of preferred stock are paid a fixed dividend before owners of common stock, but the amount of the dividend doesn't usually grow if the company grows.

Strike price: A price at which the stock or commodity underlying a call or put option can be purchased (in the case of a call) or sold (for a put) over the specified period. For instance, a call contract may allow the buyer to purchase 1,000 shares of ABC at any time in the next three months at an exercise (strike) price of $75.

CHAPTER 3

Option Basics

SUMMARY

In order to become a successful options trader, one must also develop an understanding of basic concepts such as option quotes, symbols, exercise and assignment, types of brokerage accounts, and the key factors that determine options prices. This chapter is designed to help build a foundation for successful options trading by providing a primer on these option basics.

Simply put, options give you the ability to control an underlying stock (or other financial instrument) that the option is written on. Each stock option controls 100 shares of the underlying stock. If you are buying an option, you will have the right, but not the obligation, to buy (in the case of a call) or sell (in the case of a put) a stock at a specific price by a certain date. Option sellers, in contrast, have the obligation to deliver (call) or purchase (put) the underlying stock at a specific price by a certain date. In other words, option buyers have rights, while option sellers have obligations and the additional risk should the option holder exercise the option. If you find a stock that you are interested in trading options on, simply ask your broker whether it has options, or access the Optionetics web site to search for option chains.

Chapter 3 of the main text also provides an in-depth discussion of the difference between put and call options. Particular attention is paid to strike prices, premiums, expiration dates, and recognizing whether an option is in-the-money, at-the-money, or out-of-the-money. These topics are extremely important to the active options trader. Initially such concepts might seem a bit cumbersome, but through time, these basic concepts will become second nature to the experienced options trader.

QUESTIONS AND EXERCISES

1. A ______________ gives the buyer the right, but not the obligation, to buy a specified number of shares or contracts of the underlying security at a predetermined price during a set period of time.
   A. Futures contract.
   B. Call option.
   C. Stock.
   D. Derivative.

2. If you sign a 12-month lease agreement with an option to buy a house at $200,000 and the seller charges $1,000 extra just for that 12-month option to buy the house, that charge is called the ______________.
   A. Strike price.
   B. Expiration.
   C. Credit.
   D. Premium.

3. True or False: Options are available on all stocks.

4. True or False: Once you own an option, you are obligated to buy or sell the underlying instrument.

5. Once an option ______________, you lose your right to buy or sell the underlying instrument at the specified price.
   A. Moves in-the-money.
   B. Moves out-of-the-money.
   C. Expires.
   D. None of the above.

6. Options when bought are done so at a ______________ to the buyer.
   A. Debit.
   B. Credit.
   C. Margin.
   D. None of the above.

7. Options when sold are done so by giving a _____________ to the seller.
   A. Debit.
   B. Credit.
   C. Margin.
   D. None of the above.

8. Options are available at numerous _____________ based on the price of the underlying instrument.
   A. Premiums.
   B. Margins.
   C. Expiration dates.
   D. Strike prices.

9. The more time until expiration, the more _____________ the premium.
   A. Expensive.
   B. Inexpensive.

10. True or False: Strike prices for stocks and indexes come only in multiples of 5.

11. Name the three possible relationships strike prices have to the current price of the underlying asset.
    1. ____
    2. ____
    3. ____

12. What is the main difference between American-style options and European-style options?

    ____

    ____

13. What are the three possible resolutions of an options contract?
    1. ____
    2. ____
    3. ____

14. If the writer of an option receives ____________, the option has been assigned and the writer is obligated to buy (or sell) the specified amount of underlying assets at the strike price from (or to) the assigned holder.
    A. A margin call.
    B. An assignment notice.
    C. An exercise notice.
    D. None of the above.

15. A stock option represents the right to buy or sell ____________ shares of the underlying stock.
    A. 50.
    B. 100.
    C. 250.
    D. 500.

16. The stock option expiration date is always the Saturday following the ____________ Friday of the expiration month.
    A. First.
    B. Second.
    C. Third.
    D. Last.

17. Strike prices for stock options come in increments of ____________ for stocks over $25 per share.
    A. $1.
    B. $2.
    C. $5.
    D. $10.

18. True or False: The strike prices and expiration dates of options contracts differ depending on the underlying instrument they represent.

19. Name the five components that make up option symbols:
    1. ____________________
    2. ____________________
    3. ____________________
    4. ____________________
    5. ____________________

20. Name the two types of options.

    1. ______________________________

    2. ______________________________

21. A ______________ gives the buyer the right (not the obligation) to buy the underlying stock shares or futures contract.

    A. Call option.

    B. Put option.

    C. Futures option contract.

    D. Stock option contract.

22. If the market price is more than your strike price, your call option is ______________.

    A. At-the-money.

    B. In-the-money.

    C. Out-of-the-money.

23. If the market price is less than your strike price, your call option is ______________.

    A. At-the-money.

    B. In-the-money.

    C. Out-of-the-money.

24. If the market price is the same as your strike price, your option is ______________.

    A. At-the-money.

    B. In-the-money.

    C. Out-of-the-money.

25. If you buy call options, you are ______________.

    A. Going long.

    B. Going short.

    C. Going delta neutral.

    D. Hedging.

26. If you sell call options, you are _____________.
    A. Going long.
    B. Going short.
    C. Going delta neutral.
    D. Hedging.

27. If you are _____________ (believe the market will rise), then you want to buy calls.
    A. Bearish.
    B. Bullish.

28. If you are _____________ (believe the market will drop), then you want to buy puts.
    A. Bearish.
    B. Bullish.

29. If you buy a call option, your risk is _____________.
    A. Unlimited.
    B. The price of the underlying.
    C. The margin of the underlying.
    D. The price of the premium.

30. If you sell a call option, your risk is _____________.
    A. Unlimited.
    B. The price of the underlying.
    C. The margin of the underlying.
    D. The price of the premium.

31. If the current price of XYZ is $50, fill in the blanks designating each strike as ITM, ATM, or OTM.

Strike Price of Option	Call Option Moneyness
70	
65	
60	
55	
50	
45	
40	
35	
30	

32. Name the two ways profits can be realized from purchasing a call option.

    1. ______________________________

    2. ______________________________

33. All the options that have the same unit of trading, expiration date, and strike price are called an ______________.

    A. Option class.
    B. Option series.
    C. Option division.
    D. Option suit.

34. A ______________ gives the buyer the right (not the obligation) to sell the underlying stock shares or futures contract.

    A. Call option.
    B. Put option.
    C. Futures option contract.
    D. Stock option contract.

35. If the market price is less than your strike price, your put option is ______________.
    A. At-the-money.
    B. In-the-money.
    C. Out-of-the-money.

36. If the market price is more than your strike price, your put option is ______________.
    A. At-the-money.
    B. In-the-money.
    C. Out-of-the-money.

37. If the market price is the same as your strike price, your put option is ______________.
    A. At-the-money.
    B. In-the-money.
    C. Out-of-the-money.

38. If you buy put options, you are ______________.
    A. Going long.
    B. Going short.
    C. Going delta neutral.
    D. Hedging.

39. If you sell put options, you are ______________.
    A. Going long.
    B. Going short.
    C. Going delta neutral.
    D. Hedging.

40. If you buy a put option, your risk is ______________.
    A. Unlimited.
    B. The price of the underlying.
    C. The margin of the underlying.
    D. The price of the premium.

41. If you sell a put option, your risk is _____________.
    A. Limited to the stock falling to zero.
    B. The price of the underlying.
    C. The margin of the underlying.
    D. The price of the premium.

42. If the current price of XYZ is $50, fill in the blanks designating each strike as ITM, ATM, or OTM.

Strike Price of Option	Put Option Moneyness
70	
65	
60	
55	
50	
45	
40	
35	
30	

MEDIA ASSIGNMENT

In order to better understand the basics of puts and calls, let's go to the Optionetics.com web site and create an option chain. First, connect to the Internet and type www.optionetics.com into the title bar of your Web browser. Next, type a symbol for the stock or index of your choice in the quote box that appears at the top of the home page. For instance, use the symbol QQQ. Finally, select "Chain" from the drop-down menu and click "Go."

After clicking "Go," an option chain for the Nasdaq 100 QQQ will appear inside your web browser. First, notice that the chain is clearly separated down the middle and consists of two groups of columns. In order to see the latest price quotes for call options on the QQQ, the strategist needs to look at the left side of the chain. To find information on QQQ puts, one would look to the right.

Next, notice that the first rows of options list the options with the shortest amount of time remaining until expiration. For instance, if you create this chain on January 1, 2005, the January 2005 options will appear at the top of the table. In addition, these options will be sorted based on strike price. As you move down the table, you will notice that the expiration dates change. The options with the most time remaining until expiration appear in the last rows of the table. The option chain also provides the option symbol, the bid price, the asking price, and the open interest for each option.

VOCABULARY LIST

American-style
Assignment
At-the-money
Automatic exercise
Credit
Debit
European-style
Exercise
Expiration date
In-the-money
Intrinsic value
Long
Moneyness
Near-the-money
Out-of-the-money
Root symbol
Series
Short
Strike price
Symbol

SOLUTIONS

1. A ______________ gives the buyer the right, but not the obligation, to buy a specified number of shares or contracts of the underlying security at a predetermined price during a set period of time.

   Answer: B—Call option.

   Discussion: A call is a type of options contract that can be purchased or sold. The owner of a call option purchases the right, but not the obligation, to buy a specified amount of the underlying security (e.g., 100 shares of XYZ stock) at a predetermined price for a specified period of time.

2. If you sign a 12-month lease agreement with an option to buy a house at $200,000 and the seller charges $1,000 extra just for that 12-month option to buy the house, that charge is called the _____________.

   Answer: D—Premium.

   Discussion: The premium is the amount paid by the option buyer and the amount received by the option seller when entering into the contract. There are seven major components that affect the premium of an option:

   1. The current price of the underlying financial instrument.
   2. The type of option (put or call).
   3. The strike price of the option in comparison to the current market price (intrinsic value).
   4. The amount of time remaining until expiration (time value).
   5. The current risk-free interest rate.
   6. The volatility of the underlying financial instrument.
   7. The dividend rate, if any, of the underlying financial instrument.

3. True or False: Options are available on all stocks.

   Answer: False.

   Discussion: Options are not available on every stock. Check with your broker or look for an option chain using www.optionetics.com to see if a stock you are interested in trading has available options.

4. True or False: Once you own an option, you are obligated to buy or sell the underlying instrument.

   Answer: False.

   Discussion: An option holder is not obligated to buy or sell the underlying instrument. The purchase of an option gives you the right—but not the obligation—to buy or sell the underlying. If you choose not to exercise it, you can simply let the option expire worthless.

5. Once an option _____________, you lose your right to buy or sell the underlying instrument at the specified price.

   Answer: C—Expires.

   Discussion: After expiration, the option ceases to exist. Therefore, the owner then has no rights and the seller has no obligation associated with the contract.

6. Options when bought are done so at a ______________ to the buyer.

   Answer: A—Debit.

   Discussion: If a trader buys an option, the cost of the option—the premium—is debited from the trader's account.

7. Options when sold are done so by giving a ______________ to the seller.

   Answer: B—Credit.

   Discussion: If a trader sells an option, the cost of the option—the premium—is credited to the trader's brokerage account. For example, the call's premium is the maximum profit available on a short option position and shows up as a credit in the trader's account.

8. Options are available at numerous ______________ based on the price of the underlying instrument.

   Answer: D—Strike prices.

   Discussion: Options are assigned various strike prices that are based on the current market price of the underlying asset. The strike price is the fixed price at which the asset underlying an option can be purchased (call) or sold (put).

9. The more time until expiration, the more ______________ the premium.

   Answer: A—Expensive.

   Discussion: An options contract with many months or years remaining until expiration will be worth more than an options contract with only a few days or weeks remaining. Stated differently, the more time remaining in the option's life, the greater the option's value and therefore the greater the option premium.

10. True or False: Strike prices for stocks and indexes come only in multiples of 5.

    Answer: False.

    Discussion: Strike prices may vary for stocks and indexes. In general, however, options are available at various strike prices at 2½-point intervals for stocks priced $25 and less, or 5-point intervals for stocks over $25.

11. Name the three possible relationships strike prices have to the current price of the underlying asset.

    Answer: In-the-money (ITM), at-the-money (ATM), out-of-the-money (OTM).

    Discussion: Moneyness refers to the option's strike price relative to the price of the underlying asset. If the strike price is equal to the price of the underlying asset, the option is said to be at-the-money. If the strike price is higher or lower than the underlying asset price, the option is either out-of-the-money or in-the-money depending on whether the option is a put or a call.

12. What is the main difference between American-style options and European-style options?

    Answer: The only difference between American and European options is when they can be exercised.

    Discussion: American-style options can be exercised at any time on or before their expiration dates. European options can be exercised only on (not before) their expiration dates. While stock options and exchange-traded funds settle American-style, most index options have the European-style settlement feature.

13. What are the three possible resolutions of an options contract?

    Answer: The options contract may expire and become worthless, be exercised by its owner, or be assigned.

    Discussion: If an out-of-the-money option is not exercised before expiration, it will become worthless. If the option is in-the-money at expiration, it will be exercised and the option seller will be faced with assignment of that option. For example, if the price of the underlying stock rises above a short call strike price before expiration, the short option will either be exercised or be assigned to an option buyer. The call option seller is then obligated to deliver 100 shares of the underlying stock to the option buyer at the short call strike price. This entails buying the underlying stock at the higher (market) price and delivering it to the option buyer at the lower (strike) price. The difference between these two prices constitutes the seller's loss and the buyer's open position profit. This can be a huge loss in fast markets, which is why we never recommend selling naked options.

14. If the writer of an option receives ____________, the option has been assigned and the writer is obligated to buy (or sell) the specified amount of underlying assets at the strike price from (or to) the assigned holder.

    Answer: C—An exercise notice.

    Discussion: Assignment will occur if the option is in-the-money near expiration. If so, the Options Clearing Corporation sends an exercise notice to a brokerage firm and the brokerage firm then delivers the notice to the option writer.

15. A stock option represents the right to buy or sell ____________ shares of the underlying stock.

    Answer: B—100.

    Discussion: Stock options are standardized to represent 100 shares of the underlying stock. Futures, in contrast, vary depending on the commodity's characteristics.

16. The stock option expiration date is always the Saturday following the ____________ Friday of the expiration month.

    Answer: C—Third.

    Discussion: Stock options expire at close of business prior to the Saturday after the third Friday of the expiration month. The last day to trade them is therefore on the third Friday of the option's expiration month.

17. Strike prices for stock options come in increments of ____________ for stocks over $25 per share.

    Answer: C—$5.

    Discussion: In most cases, stocks with market prices of $25 or more will have strike prices spaced at 5-point increments.

18. True or False: The strike prices and expiration dates of options contracts differ depending on the underlying instrument they represent.

    Answer: True.

    Discussion: Different underlying assets (stocks, indexes, futures, etc.) have different specifications for their respective options contracts. To find the current information regarding a contract, check the web site of the exchange where the contract is listed for trading, or go to www.optionetics.com and enter the stock symbol, then click on Option Chain.

19. Name the five components that make up option symbols.

    Answer: Underlying financial instrument, root symbol, expiration month, strike price, option type.

    Discussion: Each options contract can be described using three factors. The first is the root symbol. Sometimes the root symbol and the underlying financial instrument are the same; for instance, IBM is the root symbol for International Business Machines (IBM). Microsoft is an example of a stock with a root symbol that is not the same as the stock. The stock symbol is MSFT, while the option symbol is MSQ. The second part of an option symbol tells the expiration and reflects whether the option is a put or a call (A through L for calls and M through X for puts). If the expiration month is January and the option is a call, the second part of the symbol is an A; if the contract is a February put, the second part of the symbol is an N. Finally, the last part of the option symbol is the strike price. The letter A is used for a strike price of 5, B for 10, C for 15, all the way up to T for 100. Therefore, the symbol for the IBM February 75 call is IBMBO.

20. Name the two types of options.

    Answer: Calls and puts.

    Discussion: Calls are options that give the buyer the right to buy an underlying asset. Puts give the buyer the right to sell the underlying asset.

21. A ______________ gives the buyer the right (not the obligation) to buy the underlying stock shares or futures contract.

    Answer: A—Call option.

    Discussion: If you exercise this type of option, you are calling the underlying security away from the option seller. Hence, the option seller is obligated to deliver 100 shares of the underlying stock to the option holder.

22. If the market price is more than your strike price, your call option is ______________.

    Answer: B—In-the-money.

    Discussion: If the strike price is below the market price, the options contract has intrinsic value because it enables the owner to purchase the underlying asset at the lower strike price. So, it is in-the-money.

23. If the market price is less than your strike price, your call option is ______________.

    Answer: C—Out-of-the-money.

    Discussion: A call option that has a strike price above the market price has no intrinsic value and is therefore out-of-the-money.

24. If the market price is the same as your strike price, your option is ______________.

    Answer: A—At-the-money

    Discussion: When the strike price is equal to the price of the underlying asset, whether puts or calls, the contract is at-the-money.

25. If you buy call options, you are ______________.

    Answer: A—Going long.

    Discussion: Anytime you buy an options contract, you are going long—even if it is a put option going long a call option is a bullish strategy.

26. If you sell call options, you are ______________.

    Answer: B—Going short.

    Discussion: Option sellers are said to be short the options contract. Going short a call option is a bearish strategy and comes with unlimited risk, which is why we never recommend selling naked options.

27. If you are ______________ (believe the market will rise), then you want to buy calls.

    Answer: B—Bullish.

    Discussion: Buying a call is a bullish strategy because it allows a trader to profit from a rise in the price of the underlying asset. A long call can also be used to predetermine how much a trader wants to pay for the underlying asset—regardless of how high the price climbs over time until the option expires. A bull expects the market to move higher. A rising market is called bullish because bulls buck up with their horns.

28. If you are ______________ (believe the market will drop), then you want to buy puts.

    Answer: A—Bearish.

    Discussion: Buying a put is a bearish strategy because it allows a trader to profit from a decline in the price of the underlying asset. A long put can also be used to predetermine how much a trader wants to receive for selling the underlying asset—regardless of how low the price falls over time until the option expires. Bears expect the underlying asset to fall. A falling market is called bearish because bears swat downward with their paws.

29. If you buy a call option, your risk is ____________.

Answer: D—The price of the premium.

Discussion: The total risk associated with buying an option is the cost of entering the agreement (the premium).

30. If you sell a call option, your risk is ____________.

Answer: A—Unlimited.

Discussion: Call option sellers enter into an obligation to sell the underlying asset at a predetermined price. If they do not already own the underlying asset and it moves higher in price, they will likely be faced with assignment and will be forced to buy the underlying asset to cover assignment. Furthermore, since there is theoretically no limit to how high an underlying asset might go, the risk associated with selling call options is theoretically unlimited.

31. If the current price of XYZ is $50, fill in the blanks designating each strike as ITM, ATM, or OTM.

Answer:

Strike Price of Option	Call Option Moneyness
70	OTM
65	OTM
60	OTM
55	OTM
50	ATM
45	ITM
40	ITM
35	ITM
30	ITM

Discussion: If the strike price is equal to the price of the underlying asset, the option is said to be at-the-money. If the strike price is higher than the underlying asset price, the call option is out-of-the-money. If the strike price is lower than the underlying asset price, the call option is in-the-money.

32. Name the two ways profits can be realized from purchasing a call option.

Answer:

1. If the underlying asset increases in price before the option expires, the holder can purchase the underlying asset at the lower strike price.
2. If the underlying asset's price increases before expiration, the value of the option increases and can be sold at a profit.

Discussion: Option owners can either exercise the options contract or close the position by selling the same number of an identical options contract. For instance, if a trader holds 10 IBM January 90 calls and IBM rises to $100, the trader can exercise the option, which would allow him or her to buy 1,000 shares of the stock for the strike price of $90 and then sell those 1,000 shares in the market for $100. Alternatively, the trader could sell 10 IBM January 90 calls and close the position at a profit without exercising the options. In both cases, since the stock has risen from $90 to $100 a share, a profit will be realized.

33. All the options that have the same unit of trading, expiration date, and strike price are called an ____________.

Answer: B—Option series.

Discussion: An option series describes the options on the same underlying asset that have the same unit of trading, strike price, and expiration date.

34. A ____________ gives the buyer the right (not the obligation) to sell the underlying stock shares or futures contract.

Answer: B—Put option.

Discussion: When exercising an options contract, the owner of a put will instruct the brokerage firm to sell (or put) the underlying asset to the option writer.

35. If the market price is less than your strike price, your put option is ____________.

Answer: B—In-the-money.

Discussion: A put option has intrinsic value when the price of the underlying asset falls below the strike price of the options contract. In that case, the option is in-the-money because it allows the holder to purchase the underlying asset at the lower strike price if exercised.

36. If the market price is more than your strike price, your put option is ______________.

    Answer: C—Out-of-the-money.

    Discussion: A put option that has a strike price below the price of the underlying asset has no intrinsic value. It is out-of-the-money.

37. If the market price is the same as your strike price, your put option is ______________.

    Answer: A—At-the-money.

    Discussion: When the strike price is equal to the underlying asset, whether puts or calls, the contract is at-the-money.

38. If you buy put options, you are ______________.

    Answer: A—Going long.

    Discussion: If you buy an option, you are going long that contract. Whether it is a put or a call doesn't matter. Going long a put option is a bearish strategy.

39. If you sell put options, you are ______________.

    Answer: B—Going short.

    Discussion: Anytime you sell an option, you are going short. Going short a put option is a bullish strategy.

40. If you buy a put option, your risk is ______________.

    Answer: D—The price of the premium.

    Discussion: The total risk associated with buying an option is the premium paid for that option. This is true whether the option is a put or a call.

41. If you sell a put option, your risk is ______________.

    Answer: A—Limited to the stock falling to zero.

    Discussion: The risk of selling puts can be substantial if the stock falls sharply and the put writer is assigned the stock. However, unlike naked call selling, the risk is not unlimited. It is limited due to the fact that the stock price cannot fall below zero.

42. If the current price of XYZ is $50, fill in the blanks designating each strike as ITM, ATM, or OTM.

Answer:

Strike Price of Option	Put Option Moneyness
70	ITM
65	ITM
60	ITM
55	ITM
50	ATM
45	OTM
40	OTM
35	OTM
30	OTM

Discussion: If the strike price is equal to the price of the underlying asset, the option is said to be at-the-money. If the strike price is higher than the underlying asset price, the put option is in-the-money. If the strike price is lower than the underlying asset price, the put is out-of-the-money.

MEDIA ASSIGNMENT

Now that we have created an option chain, let's make a few observations. First, notice that the premiums of the calls with the same expiration date but different strike prices decrease as you move down the table. Why is that? In contrast, the prices of the puts *increase* as you move down the table.

Can you identify the at-the-money options? Also, notice that the premiums of the options with the same strike price but different expiration dates are different. The option with the shortest amount of time left until expiration has the smallest premium. Furthermore, in every case, the bid is less than the ask (offer) price. Do you remember what the difference between the bid and ask price is? As you probably recall, this is known as the bid-ask spread.

Once you clearly understand an option chain, the various elements, and why the prices vary among the options contracts, you probably have developed a good understanding of the options basics. So, it's time to move on to the next chapter and the discussion of basic trading strategies.

VOCABULARY DEFINITIONS

American-style: An options contract that settles American-style can be exercised at any time prior to expiration. Stock options settle American-style.

Assignment: The receipt of an exercise notice by an option writer that requires him or her to sell (in the case of a call) or purchase (in the case of a put) the underlying security at the specified strike price.

At-the-money: Refers to an option with an exercise or strike price that is equal, or almost equal, to the current market price of the underlying security.

Automatic exercise: An exercise by the clearing firm in which the firm automatically exercises an in-the-money option at expiration.

Credit: Amount that is added to the trading account when an options trader collects a premium for selling options.

Debit: The amount that is subtracted from a trader's account when a trade involves the net purchase of options contracts.

European-style: An option contract that can be exercised only on the expiration date.

Exercise: To implement the right of the holder of an option to buy (in the case of a call) or sell (in the case of a put) the underlying security. When you exercise an option, you carry out the terms of an option contract.

Expiration date: The day when the options contract expires. For stock options, the expiration date falls on close of business prior to the Saturday following the third Friday of the expiration month.

In-the-money: Refers to an options contract that has intrinsic value. A call is in-the-money if the strike price is less than the market price. A put is in-the-money if the strike price is greater than the market price of the underlying security.

Intrinsic value: The amount by which an option is in-the-money. Out-of-the-money options have no intrinsic value. To calculate the intrinsic value of a call option, take the price of the underlying and subtract the strike price. A put option's intrinsic value equals the strike price minus the price of the underlying.

Long: Buying an investment security. Traders will go long when they expect the instrument to increase in value.

Moneyness: A term to define whether an options contract is in-the-money, at-the-money, or out-of-the-money.

Near-the-money: Refers to an option with a strike price that is almost equal to the current market price of the underlying security.

Out-of-the-money: Refers to an options contract that has no intrinsic value; for instance, a call option whose exercise price is above the current market price of the underlying security or futures contract.

Root symbol: The first part of an options symbol that represents the underlying security. For instance, the root symbol for International Business Machines is IBM.

Series: All option contracts of the same class that also have the same unit of trade, expiration date, and exercise price.

Short: Selling an investment security in anticipation that the price will fall.

Strike price: A price at which the stock or commodity underlying a call or put option can be purchased (call) or sold (put) over the specified period.

Symbol: A three-, four-, or five-letter sequence that denotes a stock, option, or futures contract.

CHAPTER 4

Basic Trading Strategies

SUMMARY

In addition to risk graphs, Chapter 4 covers the following eight strategies: long stock, short stock, long call, short call, covered call, long put, short put, and covered put. These are the basic strategies that almost all options traders first learn. In fact, many options traders begin as stock traders. From there, many move on to shorting stocks or long calls. These strategies, while simple and widely used, form the basis for many more complex trading strategies, which are covered in detail in later chapters.

Before initiating any options trade, the strategist needs to determine the trade's potential risks and rewards. A risk profile can be generated to provide a graphical representation of the overall risk of a specific trade. By visualizing the potential risk and reward, a trader can find promising trades and identify potential pitfalls.

QUESTIONS AND EXERCISES

1. Every trade you place has a corresponding ____________ that graphically shows your potential risk and potential reward over a range of prices and time periods.
   A. Risk curve.
   B. Risk graph.
   C. Risk profile.
   D. All of the above.

2. Reading a risk profile is pretty easy. The horizontal numbers at the bottom of the chart read from left to right showing the ________________.

   A. Market price.

   B. Option premium price.

   C. Profit and loss.

   D. Change in overall position delta.

3. The vertical numbers from top to bottom show ________________.

   A. Market price.

   B. Option premium price.

   C. Profit and loss.

   D. Change in overall position delta.

4. Label each risk graph with the correct strategy: long stock, long call, long put, short stock, short call, short put.

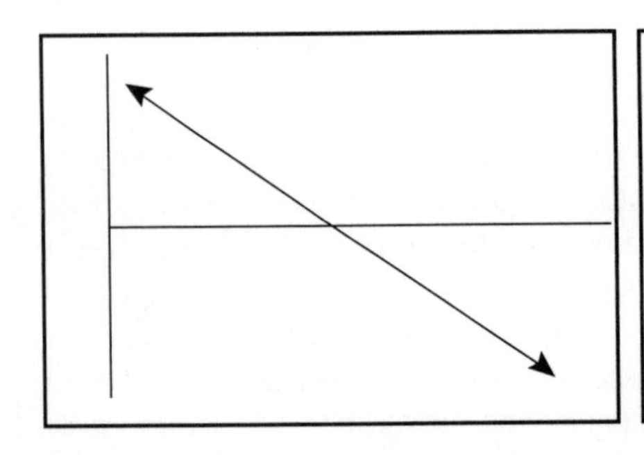

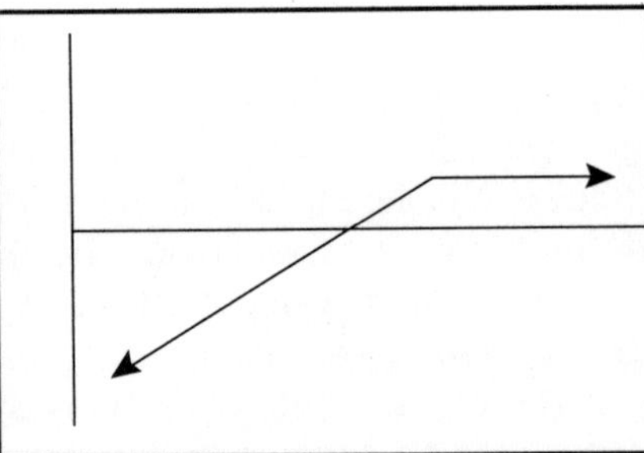

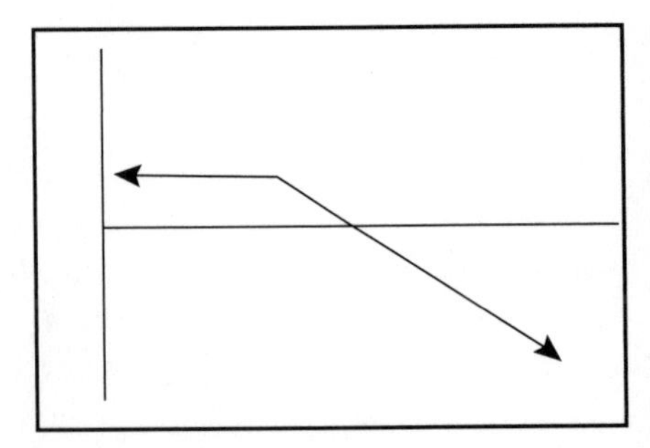

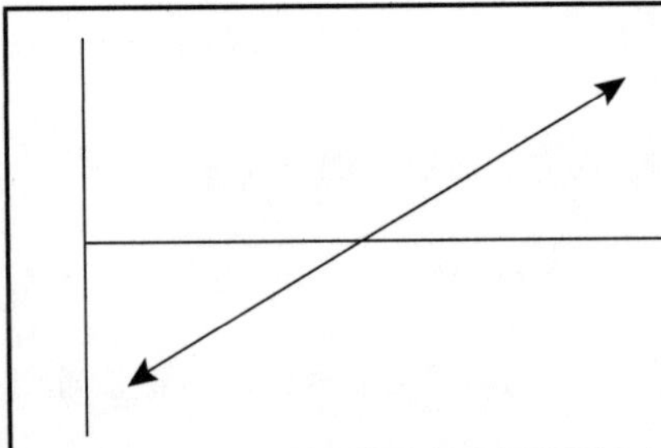

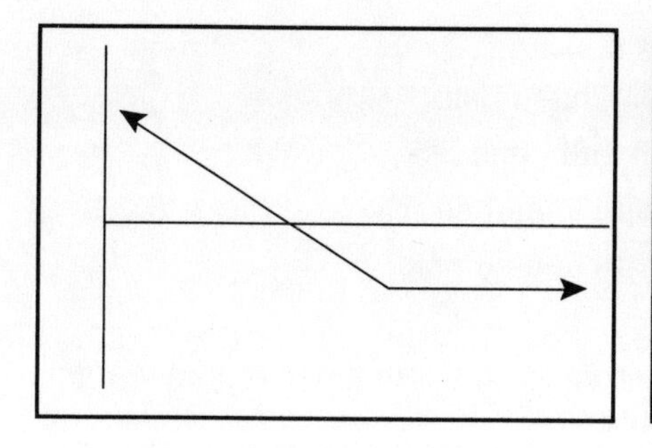
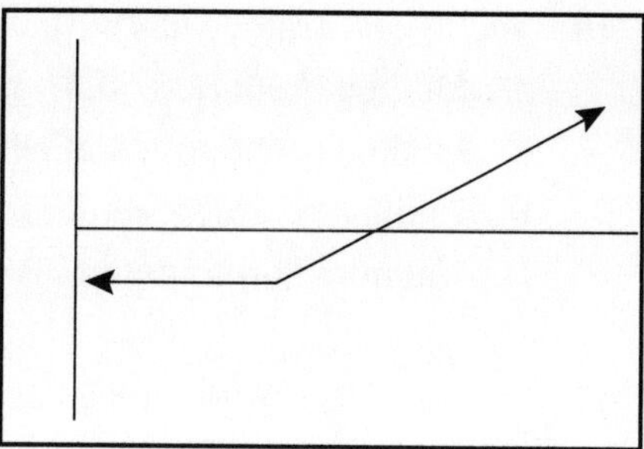

5. The long stock strategy provides ____________.
   A. Limited profit potential with limited risk.
   B. Limited profit potential with unlimited risk.
   C. Unlimited profit potential with unlimited risk.
   D. Unlimited profit potential with limited risk.

6. A stock does not have premium or time decay. It has a ____________ movement in price versus risk and reward.
   A. 1-to-1.
   B. 1-to-2.
   C. 1-to-10.
   D. 1-to-100.

7. True or False: In a short stock strategy, when the stock price falls, you make money; when it rises, you lose money.

8. A short stock strategy has ____________.
   A. Limited profit potential with limited risk.
   B. Limited profit potential with unlimited risk.
   C. High profit potential with unlimited risk.
   D. High profit potential with limited risk.

9. True or False: With a long call strategy, when the price of the underlying asset rises you make money; when it falls, you lose money.

10. A long call strategy has virtually ____________.
    A. Limited profit potential with limited risk.
    B. Limited profit potential with unlimited risk.
    C. Unlimited profit potential with unlimited risk.
    D. Unlimited profit potential with limited risk.

11. True or False: With a long call strategy, you still have to hold margin in your account to place the trade.

12. If you bought a September IBM 105 call for a premium of 5, your minimum risk on this trade would be ____________.
    A. $50 plus commissions.
    B. $100 plus commissions.
    C. $500 plus commissions.
    D. $1,000 plus commissions.

13. The breakeven for a long call at expiration is computed by ____________.
    A. Adding the cost of the call option to its strike price.
    B. Adding cost of the option to the price of the commission.
    C. Subtracting the strike price from the option premium.
    D. Subtracting the option premium from the strike price.

14. True or False: With a short call strategy, when the underlying instrument's price rises, you make money; when it falls, you lose money.

15. A short call strategy has ____________.
    A. Limited profit potential with limited risk.
    B. Limited profit potential with unlimited risk.
    C. Unlimited profit potential with unlimited risk.
    D. Unlimited profit potential with limited risk.

16. True or False: With a long put strategy, when the underlying instrument's price falls, you make money; when it rises, you lose money.

17. A long put strategy has virtually ____________.
    A. Limited profit potential with limited risk.
    B. Limited profit potential with unlimited risk.
    C. Unlimited profit potential with unlimited risk.
    D. Unlimited profit potential with limited risk.

18. The breakeven of a long put option by expiration is derived by ____________.
    A. Adding the cost of the option to its strike price.
    B. Adding the cost of the option to the price of the commission.
    C. Subtracting the strike price from the option premium.
    D. Subtracting the option premium from its strike price.

19. True or False: In a short put strategy, when the underlying instrument's price falls, you make money; when it rises, you lose money.

20. A short put strategy has ____________.
    A. Limited profit potential with limited risk.
    B. Limited profit potential with significant risk.
    C. Unlimited profit potential with significant risk.
    D. Unlimited profit potential with limited risk.

MEDIA ASSIGNMENT

This media assignment requires a piece of graph paper and an Internet connection. Once your PC is booted and online, type www.cboe.com into the Web browser, which will take you to the Chicago Board Options Exchange web site. From the CBOE home page, click on the "Trading Tools" tab, then the "Volatility Optimizer," and then click on "Options Calculator." Next select "American" in the style box. (*Note:* If for some reason the CBOE site is not available, readers can use any options calculator to complete this assignment.)

On a piece of graph paper (or a printout of an Excel spreadsheet), create a risk graph by drawing a horizontal axis and a vertical axis. Along the horizontal axis, write the numbers 60, 65, 70, 75, 80, 85, and 90 at evenly spaced intervals. From bottom to top, write the numbers 0, 1, 2, . . . , 20 along the vertical axis. Now, go back to the options calculator.

Using the chart and the options calculator, let's create a risk curve for a long call strategy. Remember that a long call is simply the purchase of a call option. So, let's input some variables into the calculator regarding this long call. First, let the strike price equal 75; the volatility is 30 percent, the annual interest rate is 5 percent, and the company pays no dividend (quarterly dividend amount equals 0). Next, in the "Days Left to Expiration" box, click "Days Until Expiration" and enter the number 100. We are going to look at an options contract with 100 days remaining until expiration, which has a strike price of 75, volatility of 30 percent, and an underlying security that pays no dividends.

Now, let's look at what happens to the call option when we change the stock price. Enter 60 into the "Equity Price" box and look at the value of the call. It is worth approximately 45 cents. On the risk graph, draw a dot at the coordinate where 60 and .45 meet (estimate .45 between 0 and 1 on the lower left-hand side of the chart). Next, plug the number 65 into the "Equity Price" box on the options calculator and notice that the value of the long call increases to roughly 1.25. Put a dot on the risk curve where 65 and 1.25 meet. Continue this process until you reach the stock price of 90. When you reach the final equity price value of 90, the long call is worth roughly 16.50. Finally, connect the dots and you have just created a risk curve for the long call. It is upward profit/loss line that slopes to the right.

In practice, the strategist would subtract the cost of the long call from the risk curve to see the true profit-and-loss potential of a long call trade. In this case, we just looked at the possible changes in the option price that result from changes in the stock price. We did not assume we purchased the long call at a specific price. If we pay, for instance, $1 for the long call, we would subtract $1 from the value of the option price. So, when the stock price is $60 a share, the loss on the trade is 55 cents: (1 – .45). However, if the stock reaches $90 a share, the gain on the trade is $15.50: (16.50 – 1).

Importantly, most options strategists do not create risk curves manually. Instead, traders rely on software packages to create the graphs. Nevertheless, to truly understand the reward/risk profile of an options trade, it is helpful to also understand how and why a risk curve has a given shape. In sum, plotting a few simple ones like the long call will help the reader better understand why various risk curves look the way they do.

VOCABULARY LIST

Breakeven

Chicago Board Options Exchange (CBOE)

Covered call

Covered put

Long call

Long put

Long stock

Options calculator

Risk curve

Risk graph

Risk profile

Short call

Short put

Short stock

SOLUTIONS

1. Every trade you place has a corresponding ____________ that graphically shows your potential risk and potential reward over a range of prices and time periods.

   Answer: D—All of the above (risk curve, risk graph, risk profile).

   Discussion: Risk curve, risk graph, and risk profile are often used interchangeably to describe a graphical representation of the risks and rewards of an options trade. Each options strategy has a corresponding risk curve that provides a simple view of the range of possible outcomes. We encourage options traders to focus on strategies that have risk curves with limited risk and high rewards, and avoid risk profiles that reflect unlimited risks and limited rewards.

2. Reading a risk profile is pretty easy. The horizontal numbers at the bottom of the chart read from left to right showing the ____________.

   Answer: A—Market price.

   Discussion: On a risk curve, the horizontal line across the bottom of the graph reflects the market price of the underlying asset.

3. The vertical numbers from top to bottom show ____________.

   Answer: C—Profit and loss.

   Discussion: A risk graph shows the price of the underlying asset along the horizontal axis and the profit or loss from the options trade along the vertical axis. If the curve is upward sloping to the right, for instance, the options strategy will show increasing profits as the underlying asset price moves higher.

4. Label each risk graph with the correct strategy: long stock, long call, long put, short stock, short call, short put.

   Answer:

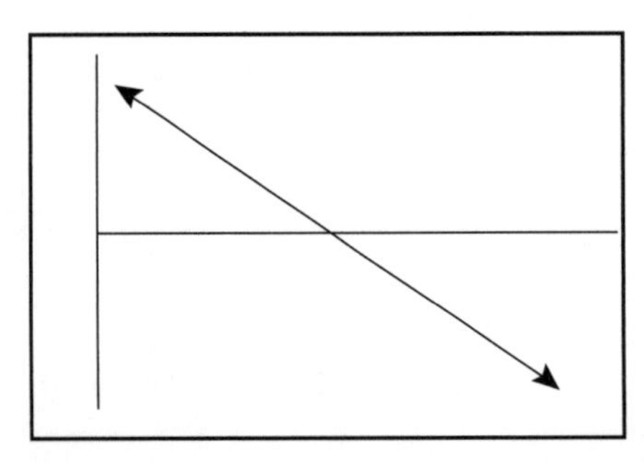

Short Stock

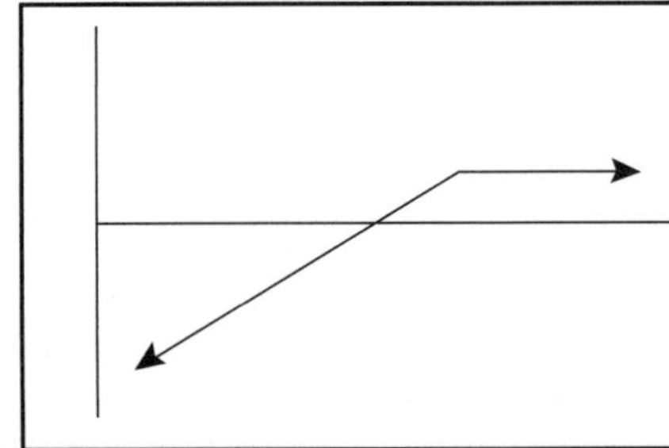

Short Put

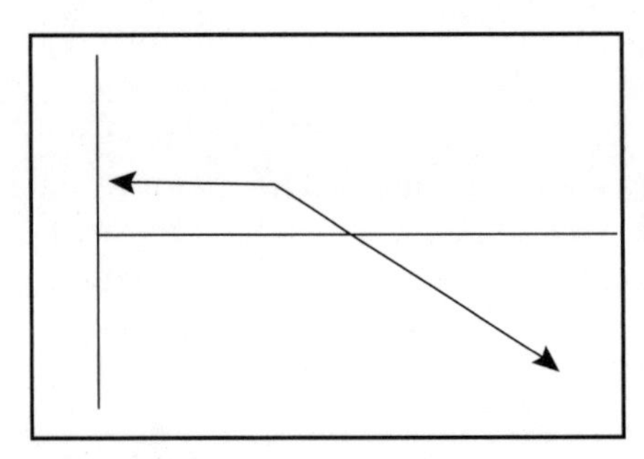

Short Call

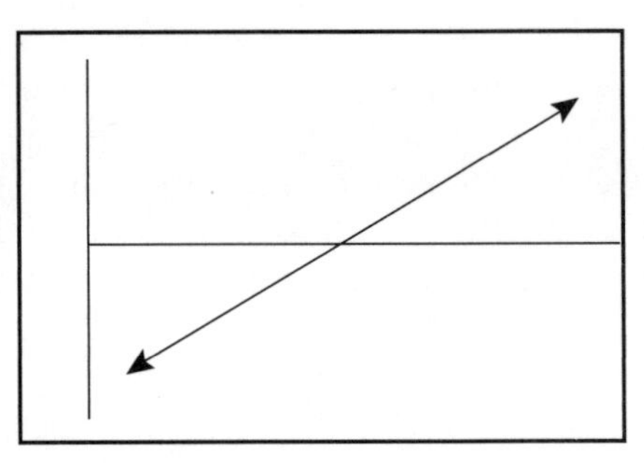

Long Stock

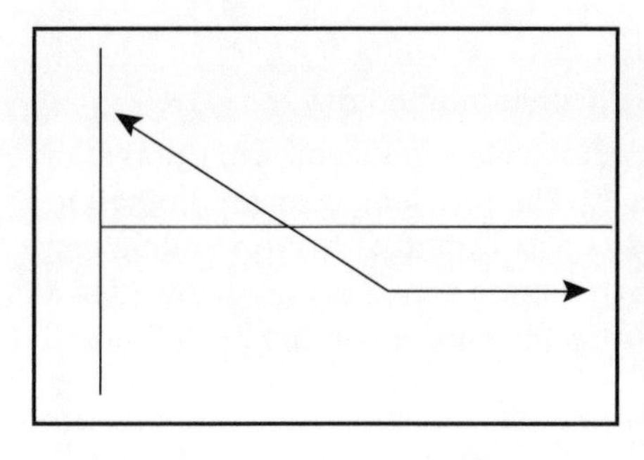

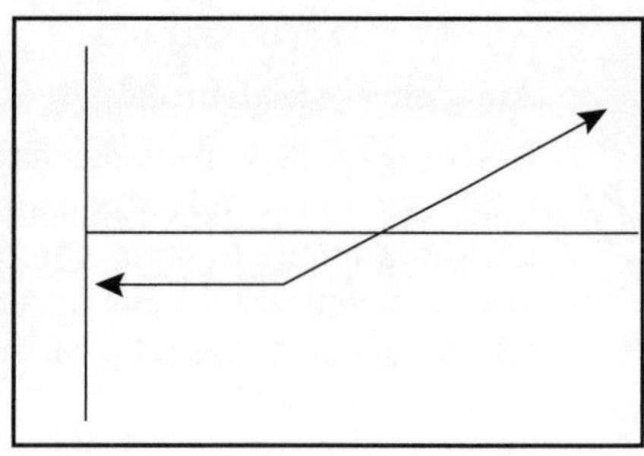

Long Put Long Call

Discussion: Each strategy has a unique risk curve that visually projects each trade's profit and loss potentials. This chapter explores the risk graphs associated with some of the most basic strategies.

5. The long stock strategy provides ______________.

   Answer: D—Unlimited profit potential with limited risk.

   Discussion: Buying stocks can involve significant risks if the stock prices move lower, but the losses will be limited to the stock falling to zero. At the same time, since there is theoretically no limit to how high a stock can climb, the profit potential associated with holding a stock is unlimited.

6. A stock does not have premium or time decay. It has a ______________ movement in price versus risk and reward.

   Answer: A—1-to-1.

   Discussion: Unlike an option, a stock does not include a premium and does not suffer from time decay. Once an investor buys shares of stock, the investor will earn $1 a share for every $1 increase in the stock price. On the other hand, if the stock falls, the investor will lose $1 a share for every $1 loss in the share price.

7. True or False: In a short stock strategy, when the stock price falls, you make money; when it rises, you lose money.

   Answer: True.

   Discussion: Shorting stock is a bearish strategy that traders use when they expect the stock price to move lower. If the stock moves higher, the short seller suffers losses.

8. A short stock strategy has ______________.

   Answer: C—High profit potential with unlimited risk.

   Discussion: Selling stocks short can have significant profit potential if the share price falls dramatically. The possible gains are limited to the stock falling to zero. The risks associated with short selling can also be significant. In fact, given that there is no ceiling to how high a stock can climb, the risks of short selling are theoretically unlimited.

9. True or False: With a long call strategy, when the price of the underlying asset rises you make money; when it falls, you lose money.

   Answer: True.

   Discussion: Call options appreciate in value as the price of the underlying asset moves higher.

10. A long call strategy has virtually ______________.

    Answer: D—Unlimited profit potential with limited risk.

    Discussion: When buying a long call, the option buyer pays a premium. If the underlying asset moves higher, the long call appreciates in value. Furthermore, since there is theoretically no limit to how high an underlying asset can go, there is unlimited profit potential. However, the risk is always limited to the premium paid for the underlying asset.

11. True or False: With a long call strategy, you still have to hold margin in your account to place the trade.

    Answer: False.

    Discussion: Zero margin borrowing is allowed, which means that you don't have to hold any margin in your account to place the trade.

12. If you bought a September IBM 105 call for a premium of 5, your total risk on this trade would be ______________.

    Answer: C—$500 plus commissions.

    Discussion: The risk inherent in buying options is limited to the premium paid. In this case, a premium of 5 means a maximum risk of $500.

13. The breakeven for a long call at expiration is computed by ______________.

    Answer: A—Adding the cost of the call option to its strike price.

    Discussion: To find the breakeven price for a long call, you take the strike price of the option and add the option premium. If the price of the underlying asset is equal to this value at expiration, the long call will (theoretically) break even.

14. True or False: With a short call strategy, when the underlying instrument's price rises, you make money; when it falls, you lose money.

    Answer: False.

    Discussion: In a short call strategy, when the underlying instrument's price falls, you make money; when it rises, you lose money.

15. A short call strategy has ______________.

    Answer: B—Limited profit potential with unlimited risk.

    Discussion: When selling calls, the profit is limited to the premium received. However, if the underlying asset makes a move higher, the short call strategy will begin to experience losses. If the stock makes a large percentage move higher, the losses can be significant.

16. True or False: With a long put strategy, when the underlying instrument's price falls, you make money; when it rises, you lose money.

    Answer: True.

    Discussion: Long puts increase in value when the underlying asset falls. If the underlying asset moves higher, the put option will experience a loss of value.

17. A long put strategy has virtually ______________.

    Answer: A—Limited profit potential with limited risk.

    Discussion: A long put will increase in value if the underlying security moves lower. The profit can be significant if the security makes a large percentage move lower. However, since the underlying asset cannot fall below zero, the potential profits are limited. The risks involved are also limited and are equal to the premium paid for the long put.

18. The breakeven of a long put option by expiration is derived by ______________.

    Answer: D—Subtracting the option premium from its strike price.

    Discussion: If the value of the underlying asset at expiration is equal to the strike price minus the premium, the long put breaks even.

19. True or False: In a short put strategy, when the underlying instrument's price falls, you make money; when it rises, you lose money.

    Answer: False.

    Discussion: Selling a put is a bullish strategy that profits when the price of the underlying asset moves higher. Oftentimes, the goal in shorting a put is to collect the premium and see the option expire worthless, which allows the put writer to keep the credit received from selling the put. The put will expire worthless if it is out-of-the-money at expiration and this will occur if the price of the underlying asset rises above the put strike price. At other times, put sellers hope to have the put assigned and take ownership of the underlying security. In either case, when the underlying asset price rises, the put seller makes money. On the other hand, when the price of the underlying asset falls, money will most likely be lost.

20. A short put strategy has ____________.

    Answer: B—Limited profit potential with significant risk.

    Discussion: Naked put selling involves significant risk if the underlying asset makes a large percentage move lower. While the risks are limited to the underlying instrument falling to zero, the short put strategy is still a very high risk aproach. The profit is also limited and is equal to the premium received for selling the put.

MEDIA ASSIGNMENT

The media assignment encourages the reader to use the free options calculator at the Chicago Board Options Exchange web site to create a risk curve. Plugging the various stock prices into the calculator produces the following values. For instance, with the stock at $80 a share, the long call would be worth $8.40.

Stock Price	Call Option Price
60	0.45
65	1.25
70	2.80
75	5.15
80	8.40
85	12.30
90	16.50

The next step is to plot the coordinates on the risk curve. For example, the first dot (in the lower left-hand corner of the risk graph) appears where the stock price equals $60 a share and the option is worth 45 cents. As we can see, the risk curve of the long call is upward sloping to the right. In later chapters, we will see how to repeat the same analysis using more complex strategies.

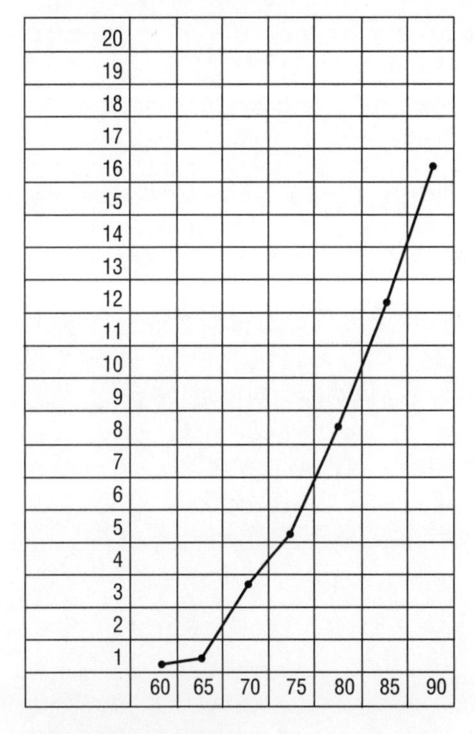

Long Call Risk Curve

VOCABULARY DEFINITIONS

Breakeven: The point where a position shows no profits and no losses. For example, if an investor sells a stock for the same price that was paid, she will break even.

Chicago Board Options Exchange (CBOE): Established in 1973, the CBOE was the first organized options exchange in the United States.

Covered call: A strategy that involves buying stock shares and selling calls. If the calls are assigned, the investor must relinquish the shares. The covered call can be established as one position or calls can be sold against an existing stock position.

Covered put: A strategy that involves selling one put against the short sale of 100 shares of stock.

Long call: The purchase of a call option in anticipation that the underlying asset will rise in price.

Long put: The purchase of a put option in anticipation that the underlying asset will decline.

Long stock: A bullish strategy that involves buying and holding shares of stock. If you buy 100 shares of XYZ, you are long XYZ.

Options calculator: A tool used by options traders to compute theoretical prices, volatility, delta, and the other so-called Greeks.

Risk curve, risk graph, and/or risk profile: A graphical representation of risk and reward on a given trade as prices change.

Short call: A bearish strategy that involves selling a call option to collect the premium.

Short put: A bullish strategy that involves selling a put option to collect the premium.

Short stock: Selling shares of stock in anticipation that the price will go down.

CHAPTER 5

Introducing Vertical Spreads

SUMMARY

In this chapter, the reader delves into the world of vertical spreads. The following four strategies are examined in depth: bull call, bull put, bear call, and bear put. An example of each strategy is included to enable the reader to witness a hands-on illustration of each specific trading technique. These strategies are used to limit risk, yet they still allow option traders to make nice profits.

Bull call and bear put spreads are debit strategies that use options with at least 90 days to expiration. Bear call and bull put spreads are credit strategies that use options that expire in less than 45 days. Since spreads involve the buying and selling of options, understanding the dynamic of the bid-ask spread is vital to your success. In order to pay the price you are willing to spend when placing a vertical spread, it's best to use a limit order inside the bid-ask spread.

Vertical spreads are great strategies to get started with as you learn the options game. However, since paper trading various vertical spreads can enable options traders to learn how to trade without losing real capital, these limited risk strategies should be paper traded before real money is put into action. After developing a strong understanding of vertical spread mechanics, a trader can use a small amount of capital to place a limited risk trade in the marketplace. Although unlimited profits cannot be made trading vertical spreads, risks are minimized, allowing traders to stay in the game longer.

QUESTIONS AND EXERCISES

1. True or False: Strategic trades are typically short-term trading opportunities geared especially for day traders and short-term traders who do not have the opportunity to monitor the markets very closely each day.

2. True or False: Long-term trades take a while to blossom and bear fruit, which gives the long-term trader more time to develop the art of patience.

3. Delta neutral trades are hedged when the total position delta equals ______________.
   A. +100.
   B. –100.
   C. +50.
   D. –50.
   E. Zero.

4. Adjustments are made by ______________ in such a way as to bring the overall trade back to delta neutral.
   A. Buying instruments.
   B. Selling instruments.
   C. Buying or selling instruments.
   D. Exiting the trade.

5. The ______________ is a high-leverage strategy consisting of going long one call at a lower strike price and short one call at a higher strike price.
   A. Bear call spread.
   B. Bear put spread.
   C. Bull call spread.
   D. Bull put spread.

6. The bull call spread has ______________.
   A. Limited profit potential with limited risk.
   B. Limited profit potential with unlimited risk.
   C. Unlimited profit potential with unlimited risk.
   D. Unlimited profit potential with limited risk.

7. Calculate the maximum reward and risk and the breakeven for the following bull call spread trade.

   Long 1 December Bank Index ($BKX) 90 Call @ 7.80

   Short 1 December BKX 100 Call @ 5.00

   Maximum reward = ______________________________

   Maximum risk = ______________________________

   Breakeven = ______________________________

8. In a ____________, you buy the lower strike put and sell the higher strike put using the same number of options.
   A. Bear call spread.
   B. Bear put spread.
   C. Bull call spread.
   D. Bull put spread.

9. A bull put spread has a ____________.
   A. Limited profit potential with limited risk.
   B. Limited profit potential with unlimited risk.
   C. Unlimited profit potential with unlimited risk.
   D. Unlimited profit potential with limited risk.

10. Calculate the maximum reward and risk and the breakeven for the following bull put spread trade.

    Long 1 June Bank Index ($BKX) 100 Put @ 6.75

    Short 1 June BKX 110 Put @ 10.50

    Maximum reward = ______________________________

    Maximum risk = ______________________________

    Breakeven = ______________________________

11. In a ____________, you sell the lower strike call and buy the higher strike call using the same number of options.
    A. Bear call spread.
    B. Bear put spread.
    C. Bull call spread.
    D. Bull put spread.

12. A bear call spread has a ___________.
    A. Limited profit potential with limited risk.
    B. Limited profit potential with unlimited risk.
    C. Unlimited profit potential with unlimited risk.
    D. Unlimited profit potential with limited risk.

13. Calculate the maximum reward and risk and the breakeven for the following bear call spread trade.

    Long 1 December IBM 90 Call @ 7.00

    Short 1 December IBM 80 Call @ 11.50

    Maximum reward = ___________________________

    Maximum risk = ___________________________

    Breakeven = ___________________________

14. In a ___________, you buy a higher strike price put and sell a lower strike price put.
    A. Covered write.
    B. Bear call spread.
    C. Bear put spread.
    D. Bull call spread.
    E. Bull put spread.

15. A bear put spread has a ___________.
    A. Limited profit potential with limited risk.
    B. Limited profit potential with unlimited risk.
    C. Unlimited profit potential with unlimited risk.
    D. Unlimited profit potential with limited risk.

16. Calculate the maximum reward and risk for the following bear put spread trade.

    Long 1 October IBM 95 Put @ 3.75

    Short 1 October IBM 90 Put @ 2.50

    Maximum reward = ___________________________

    Maximum risk = ___________________________

    Breakeven = ___________________________

MEDIA ASSIGNMENT

Vertical spreads offer predetermined risks and rewards. Understanding the risks of a trade is vital to the success of an options trader. In this exercise, using the Internet take the time to create various trades with their corresponding risk graphs of the four different types of trades mentioned in this chapter. We will discuss risk graphs in more detail later, but search the Internet and the Optionetics site to learn all you can about the risk graphs for the four types of trades talked about in this chapter: bull call spread, bear put spread, bull put spread, and bear call spread.

VOCABULARY LIST

Ask
At-the-money (ATM)
Bear call spread
Bear put spread
Bull call spread
Bull put spread
Bid
Bid-asked spread
Credit spread
Debit spread
In-the-money (ITM)
Intrinsic value
Leg in
Limit order
Out-of-the-money (OTM)
Slippage
Time value
Vertical spread

SOLUTIONS

1. True or False: Strategic trades are typically short-term trading opportunities geared especially for day traders and short-term traders who do not have the opportunity to monitor the markets very closely each day.

   Answer: False.

   Discussion: Strategic trades are short-term trading opportunities that are geared for traders who *do* have the time to monitor the markets closely each day.

2. True or False: Long-term trades take a while to blossom and bear fruit, which gives the long-term trader more time to develop the art of patience.

   Answer: True.

Discussion: There is a place for long-term trades, especially for those who cannot spend a lot of time watching the market. The longer-term the trade, the more fundamental analysis comes into play. However, technical analysis can still be used for entry and exit points. Though long-term trades provide more leeway to be right, a trader should still stick with appropriate exit points.

3. Delta neutral trades are hedged when the total position delta equals ____________.

   Answer: E—Zero.

   Discussion: As the name implies, we want to have the overall delta as close to zero as possible for delta neutral trades. When the delta strays from zero, a trade is then showing a directional bias. Many experienced traders like to use delta neutral strategies like long synthetic straddles so adjustments can be made along the way to bring in additional profits and return the trade to delta neutral.

4. Adjustments are made by ____________ in such a way as to bring the overall trade back to delta neutral.

   Answer: C—Buying or selling instruments.

   Discussion: In this chapter, the main text discusses the given delta for different types of securities and options. By understanding the approximate delta for an option, traders can make adjustments that shift the trade back to delta neutral. For example, if a synthetic straddle has moved higher and you are long the stock and long two ATM puts, you would have a few choices: You could sell shares of stock to bring in some profits or add more puts. Of course, always view a risk graph before making a final decision on what adjustments should be made.

5. The ____________ is a high-leverage strategy consisting of going long one call at a lower strike price and short one call at a higher strike price.

   Answer: C—Bull call spread.

   Discussion: By purchasing a lower strike call and selling a higher strike call, a trader creates a debit strategy, which becomes the maximum risk in the trade. The cost of the trade is lowered by selling the higher strike call, although the reward is also limited. Using a bull call spread allows a trader to be wrong about the direction of the underlying security yet experience only a minor loss.

6. The bull call spread has ______________.

   Answer: A—Limited profit potential with limited risk.

   Discussion: Many new traders do not initially understand the benefits of a bull call spread because the reward is limited. However, by examining various outcomes for a bull call spread, a trader will see how this strategy provides downside protection. Most successful traders have a specific profit goal in mind, so it usually isn't a big issue to have limited rewards. If a trader expects the underlying to rise sharply, then a straight call or a fairly wide bull call spread should be used.

7. Calculate the maximum reward and risk and the breakeven for the following bull call spread trade.

   Long 1 December Bank Index ($BKX) 90 Call @ 7.80

   Short 1 December BKX 100 Call @ 5.00

   Answer:

   Maximum reward = [(100 – 90) – 2.80] × 100 = $720 [(Difference in strikes – net debit) × 100].

   Maximum risk = (7.80 – 5.00) × 100 = $280 (Net debit).

   Breakeven = (90 + 2.80) = 92.80 (Lower strike price + net debit).

   Discussion: The maximum risk is always the net debit for a bull call spread. We normally want to see a maximum profit that is at least twice as high as the maximum risk. Thus, if we spend $150 for a bull call spread, we want to be able to possibly make at least $300. A trader should always create a risk graph before entering a trade to see where the maximum reward, maximum risk, and breakeven points fall. Traders can create bull call spreads that have large reward-to-risk ratios; but if the breakeven needs to see a very large move, this might tell us that the trade is not worth it.

8. In a ______________, you buy the lower strike put and sell the higher strike put using the same number of options.

   Answer: D—Bull put spread.

   Discussion: A bull put spread is a credit spread composed of selling the higher strike put and buying the lower strike put. However, because a bull put spread profits as long as the underlying closes above the higher strike, this strategy can benefit the trader in a large number of situations. In general, if we sell an ATM put, the underlying can trade sideways or higher and we still would receive the maximum profit (the net credit). The high probability of success does come with higher risk in the event the underlying moves lower.

9. A bull put spread has a ______________.

   Answer: A—Limited profit potential with limited risk.

   Discussion: Just like a debit spread, a credit spread has limited reward and limited risk. However, a bull put spread's higher probability of success also means a larger risk. Nonetheless, the risk is limited and credit spread traders can make substantial profits using this strategy.

10. Calculate the maximum reward and risk and the breakeven for the following bull put spread trade.

    Long 1 June Bank Index ($BKX) 100 Put @ 6.75

    Short 1 June BKX 110 Put @ 10.50

    Answer:

    Maximum reward = (10.50 – 6.75) × 100 = $375 (Net credit).

    Maximum risk = [(110 – 100) – 3.75] × 100 = $625 [(Difference in strikes – net credit)] × 100].

    Breakeven = 110 – 3.75 = 106.25 (Higher strike price – net credit).

    Discussion: A bull put spread is created by combining the sale of a higher strike put with the purchase of a lower strike put. The goal is to see the underlying asset move higher and for both puts to expire worthless. If so, the strategist will keep the net credit, which is also the maximum reward. Since a credit spread has a higher success rate than a debit spread, the amount at risk normally will often be higher than the possible reward. However, over time, a credit spread trader should see substantially more wins than losses. As with any strategy, it is important to look at a risk graph of the trade before entering to make sure the reward, risk, and breakeven all fit your outlook for the stock.

11. In a ______________, you sell the lower strike call and buy the higher strike call using the same number of options.

    Answer: A—Bear call spread.

    Discussion: As the name implies, a bear call spread is bearish in nature, but uses calls to create a credit. As long as the underlying security closes at expiration below the lower strike call, the entire net premium becomes a profit. This means that we can enter a bear call spread when we think the stock is going to trade sideways or move slightly lower by expiration.

12. A bear call spread has a _____________.

    Answer: A—Limited profit potential with limited risk.

    Discussion: I believe in limiting risk in every situation, and for this reason I never suggest selling naked options. Instead of selling a naked call, you may want to consider limiting your risk by entering a credit spread. Yes, the reward is also lowered, but this keeps a trader in the game without losing large amounts of capital on a trade gone bad.

13. Calculate the maximum reward and risk and the breakeven for the following bear call spread trade.

    Long 1 December IBM 90 Call @ 7.00

    Short 1 December IBM 80 Call @ 11.50

    Answer:

    Maximum reward = (11.50 – 7.00) × 100 = $450 (Net credit).

    Maximum risk = [(90 – 80) – 4.50] × 100 = $550 [(Difference between strikes – net credit) × 100].

    Breakeven = 80 + 4.50 = 84.50 (Lower strike price + net credit).

    Discussion: If IBM were to close at or below $80 at expiration, then this trade would achieve a maximum profit of $450. The maximum profit is equal to the credit received. The risk is calculated by subtracting the net credit from the distance between strikes. The breakeven is found by adding the net credit received to the lower strike. In this case, we need IBM to close at $84.50 or below to see a profit.

14. In a _____________, you buy a higher strike price put and sell a lower strike price put.

    Answer: C—Bear put spread.

    Discussion: Using *bear* and *put* together conveys the bearish bias of a debit spread. The idea is that we can lower the cost of buying a straight put by selling a lower strike put. Though this limits the maximum profit, it also lessens the trade's risk. If the underlying moves higher, a spread is going to see a much smaller loss than a straight put.

15. A bear put spread has a _____________.

    Answer: A—Limited profit potential with limited risk.

    Discussion: Sale of a lower strike put lowers the initial debit, but also reduces the reward. A straight put makes money as the underlying falls all the way to zero. However, a bear put spread is a limited reward, limited risk strategy. If you expect the stock to fall sharply, you might be better served using a straight put. If you predetermine your exit price, then using a debit spread might work best.

16. Calculate the maximum reward and risk for the following bear put spread trade.

    Long 1 October IBM 95 Put @ 3.75

    Short 1 October IBM 90 Put @ 2.50

    Maximum reward = [(95 – 90) – 1.25] × 100 = $375 [(Difference in strikes – net debit) × 100].

    Maximum risk = (3.75 – 2.50) × 100 = $125 (Net debit).

    Breakeven = (95 – 1.25) = 93.75 (Higher strike price – net debit).

    Discussion: The maximum risk for a bear put spread is the initial debit to enter the trade. Since a bear put spread combines the sale of a put with the purchase of a higher strike put, the net debit will be lower than when buying a straight put. The maximum reward in this example takes place if IBM closes at or below 90 at expiration. In this case, a profit of $375 occurs. This is calculated by subtracting the initial debit from the difference in strike prices. The breakeven point is calculated by subtracting the net debit from the higher strike. Thus, the trade makes a profit if IBM closes at or below $93.75 at expiration.

MEDIA ASSIGNMENT

When it comes to trading, practice really does make perfect. To learn the inner workings of the four strategies described in this chapter, take advantage of the My Portfolio section of the Optionetics web site to set up and track vertical spread trades. Just register at the site and you're ready to start searching for promising trades that will enable you to learn how these strategies work using real-world markets.

In addition, the Optionetics web site has hundreds of insightful articles about a multitude of topics that can be reviewed. Use the article search feature to find articles about the various vertical spreads. Though many articles will have a recurring theme, we often learn best by repetition and slight variances in the way a topic is taught. Traders can also use the discussion boards on the Optionetics web site to get feedback and information from other traders as well as from various Optionetics writers and instructors.

VOCABULARY DEFINITIONS

Ask: The lowest price acceptable to a prospective seller of a security. A low demand for a stock translates to the market being offered down to the lowest price at which a person is willing to sell. Off-floor traders buy at the ask price and sell at the bid price. Together, the bid and ask prices constitute a quotation or quote, and the difference between the two prices is the bid-ask spread. The bid-ask dynamic is common to all stocks and options.

At-the-money (ATM): When the strike price of an option is the same as the current price of the underlying instrument.

Bear call spread: A strategy in which a trader sells a lower strike call and buys a higher strike call to create a trade with limited profit and limited risk. A fall in the price of the underlying increases the value of the spread. Net credit transaction; maximum loss = difference between the strike prices less net credit; maximum gain = net credit.

Bear put spread: A strategy in which a trader sells a lower strike put and buys a higher strike put to create a trade with limited profit and limited risk. A fall in the price of the underlying increases the value of the spread. Net debit transaction; maximum loss = net debit; maximum gain = difference between strike prices less the net debit.

Bull call spread: A strategy in which a trader buys a lower strike call and sells a higher strike call to create a trade with limited profit and limited risk. A rise in the price of the underlying increases the value of the spread. Net debit transaction; maximum loss = net debit; maximum gain = difference between strike prices less the net debit.

Bull put spread: A strategy in which a trader sells a higher strike put and buys a lower strike put to create a trade with limited profit and limited risk. A rise in the price of the underlying increases the value of the spread. Net credit transaction; maximum loss = difference between strike prices less credit; maximum gain = net credit.

Bid: The bid is the highest price a prospective buyer is prepared to pay for a trading unit of a specified security. If there is a high demand for the underlying asset, the prices are bid up to a higher level. Off-floor traders sell at the bid price and buy at the ask price.

Bid-asked spread: The difference between bid and offer prices. The term *asked* is usually used in over-the-counter trading. The term *offered* is used in exchange trading. The bid and asked, or offered, prices together comprise a quotation, or quote.

Credit spread: The difference in value of two options, where the value of the one sold exceeds the value of the one purchased to create a net credit for the combined position.

Debit spread: The difference in value of two options, where the value of the long position exceeds the value of the short position to create a net debit for the combined position.

In-the-money (ITM): If you were to exercise an option and it would generate a profit at the time, it is known to be in-the-money. A call option is in-the-money if the strike price is less than the market price of the underlying security. A put option is in-the-money if the strike price is greater than the market price of the underlying security.

Intrinsic value: The amount by which a market is in-the-money. Out-of-the-money options have no intrinsic value. Call Intrinsic value = underlying – strike price. Put Intrinsic value = strike price – underlying.

Leg in: When a trader enters each part of a spread separately instead of entering the trade as one order with his or her broker.

Limit order: An order to buy a stock at or below a specified price or to sell a stock at or above a specified price. For instance, you could tell a broker, "Buy me 100 shares of XYZ Corporation at $8 or less" or "Sell 100 shares of XYZ at $10 or better."

Out-of-the-money (OTM): Refers to an option whose exercise price has no intrinsic value. A call option is out-of-the-money if its exercise or strike price is above the current market price of the underlying security. A put option is out-of-the-money if its exercise or strike price is below the current market price of the underlying security.

Slippage: The difference between estimated transaction costs and actual transaction costs. The difference is usually composed of price revisions or spread and commission costs.

Time value: The amount by which the current market price of an option exceeds its intrinsic value. The intrinsic value of a call is the amount by which the market price of the underlying security exceeds the strike price at which the option may be exercised. The intrinsic value of a put is calculated as the amount by which the market price of the underlying security is below the exercise price.

Vertical spread: A spread in which one option is bought and one option is sold, where the options are of the same type, have the same underlying, and have the same expiration date, but have different strike prices.

CHAPTER 6

Demystifying Delta

SUMMARY

In this chapter, the reader is introduced to the basics of delta neutral trading. Two of the most important market characteristics—volatility and liquidity—are discussed at length. In addition, the Greek options term *delta* is explored in detail and the mechanics of delta neutral trading are introduced. In order to utilize the various strategies that can be created using options, futures, and stock, traders need to understand how volatility and liquidity impact these trading tools.

Delta neutral trading is a common way for floor traders to minimize risk. However, retail traders can also use delta neutral strategies to make profits while minimizing risk. In order to fully understand delta neutral trading, traders must develop a strong understanding of delta and how it is calculated. In general, long calls and short puts have positive deltas, whereas short calls and long puts have negative deltas. One hundred shares of stock correspond to a fixed delta of plus 100 deltas when purchased and minus 100 deltas when sold short. A delta neutral trade combines long and short deltas to create an overall position delta of zero.

QUESTIONS AND EXERCISES

1. Locating opportunities for delta neutral trades depends on finding markets with ____________.
   A. High liquidity and high volatility.
   B. High liquidity and low volatility.
   C. Low liquidity and high volatility.
   D. Low liquidity and low volatility.

2. True or False: The higher an asset's volatility, the higher the prices of its options.

3. A market's ____________ can be defined as the amount of volume that enables a trader to buy or sell a security or derivative and receive fair value for it.
   A. Volatility.
   B. Equilibrium level.
   C. Support.
   D. Liquidity.

4. True or False: Delta neutral strategies are suitable for day trading.

5. A stock option's delta can be calculated by ____________ and multiplying by 100.
   A. Dividing the change in the premium by the change in the price of the underlying.
   B. Dividing the change in the price of the underlying by the change in the premium.
   C. Multiplying the change in the premium by the change in the price of the underlying.
   D. Multiplying the change in the price of the underlying by the change in the premium.

6. One hundred shares of stock have fixed deltas of ____________.
   A. Plus 50.
   B. Minus 50.
   C. Plus or minus 50.
   D. Plus or minus 100.

7. Long call options have ______________ deltas.
   A. Positive.
   B. Negative.

8. Short put options have ______________ deltas.
   A. Positive.
   B. Negative.

9. As a rule of thumb, the deeper ______________ your option is, the higher the delta.
   A. In-the-money.
   B. Out-of-the-money.

10. ______________ options have a delta of plus or minus 50.
    A. In-the-money.
    B. Out-of-the-money.
    C. At-the-money.

11. When an option is very deep ______________, it will start acting very much like the underlying stock.
    A. In-the-money.
    B. Out-of-the-money.
    C. At-the-money.

MEDIA ASSIGNMENT

Understanding how delta impacts a trade is vital to learning how to trade delta neutral. Though there are many trading-related web sites, there aren't many sites that provide the delta for an option. If you have access to the Optionetics Platinum site or if you use an options program from another source, take the time to learn about delta. If you don't have any of these, you can use an options calculator to figure the delta of an option. Your assignment is to look at different options and decide what delta you think would be associated with that option. After you have done this with several options, check the actual data to see how close you were. After a while, you'll be surprised how accurate your initial decision about the delta is compared with the actual delta.

VOCABULARY LIST

Delta

Derivatives

Liquidity

Long-term equity anticipation securities (LEAPS)

Position delta

Skew

Tick

Volatility

SOLUTIONS

1. Locating opportunities for delta neutral trades depends on finding markets with ____________.

   Answer: A—High liquidity and high volatility.

   Discussion: Delta neutral trades rely on magnitude of movement in the underlying security. High volatility often scares away new traders; but an experienced trader usually thrives on volatility. When a stock or an index shows a lot of movement, this volatility enables delta neutral traders to make profits even while minimizing risk. However, in order to take advantage of high volatility, a trader must understand the characteristics of volatility and delta. High liquidity is also needed to get your order filled at a good price when entering and exiting a trade.

2. True or False: The higher an asset's volatility, the higher the prices of its options.

   Answer: True.

   Discussion: Volatility tells a trader how much the stock is expected to move. This means the higher the volatility, the greater the chance of a move of sufficient magnitude in the underlying asset. An option premium is like an insurance premium, which means we pay more when there is more associated risk. If volatility is high, the stock is expected to move a great deal more; thus the premium to enter a call or put is higher. A delta neutral trader thrives on high volatility, as it increases the chances of market moves of high magnitude, which provides for a number of profit-making opportunities.

3. A market's _____________ can be defined as the amount of volume that enables a trader to buy or sell a security or derivative and receive fair value for it.

   Answer: D—Liquidity.

   Discussion: When a stock or option has low liquidity, the price tends to be skewed. Retail traders buy at the ask and sell at the bid, so it is important to find options with high liquidity so the bid-ask spread is not too wide. Slippage is the amount of money lost by buying at the ask and selling at the bid. With options that have low liquidity, the spread will often be large and it will be difficult to get fair value for the options.

4. True or False: Delta neutral strategies are suitable for day trading.

   Answer: False.

   Discussion: Though delta neutral trades are used by floor traders to hedge risk, it is usually not suitable to day trade this type of strategy. I recommend trying to reduce risk and stress by utilizing delta neutral trading techniques over a longer trading period.

5. An option's delta can be calculated by _____________ and multiplying by 100.

   Answer: A—Dividing the change in the premium by the change in the price of the underlying.

   Discussion: Options are derivatives, so their price is derived from the movement of the underlying security. Delta measures the move in an option's price as compared to a move in the underlying security. For example, if a stock moves $1 and the option moves higher by $0.50, then the delta is considered to be 50. An ATM option normally has a delta near 50, with ITM options seeing higher deltas and OTM options seeing lower deltas. A delta of 50 means that the underlying has a 50 percent chance of becoming in-the-money by expiration.

6. One hundred shares of stock have fixed deltas of _____________.

   Answer: D—Plus or minus 100.

   Discussion: One hundred shares of long stock have a delta of +100. One hundred shares of short stock have a delta of –100. No matter how the stock price fluctuates, the delta of plus or minus 100 will remain fixed. It is important to understand what the delta is for different securities so that combinations can be formed to create delta neutral trades.

7. Long call options have _____________ deltas.

   Answer: A—Positive.

   Discussion: A long call would have a delta between 0 and 100. A long call can't have a delta higher than 100 because the most a call option can move is point-for-point with the underlying security. The deeper ITM the call option gets, the closer to 100 the delta will become. The farther OTM the option gets, the closer to zero the delta gets.

8. Short put options have _____________ deltas.

   Answer: A—Positive.

   Discussion: With a short put, a trader profits as the stock moves higher, and this means the delta is positive. (A long put would have a negative delta because the option makes money as the underlying declines.) Though in general Optionetics doesn't advocate trading short puts, or any naked options, there are times when using these types of options is advisable to create delta neutral trades.

9. As a rule of thumb, the deeper _____________ your option is, the higher the delta.

   Answer: A—In-the-money.

   Discussion: As an option moves deeper in-the-money, it starts to mirror the movement of the underlying. A very deep ITM option will have very little time value and will start to trade nearly point-for-point with the underlying security. The opposite also holds true: An option that is far OTM will see little movement for each point move in the underlying security.

10. _____________ options have a delta of plus or minus 50.

    Answer: C—At-the-money.

    Discussion: In most cases, ATM options have a delta that is very close to 50. Another way of looking at this is to say that an ATM option has a 50/50 proposition of finishing in-the-money. A straddle is a common delta neutral strategy that uses an ATM put and an ATM call, which produces an overall delta near zero.

11. When an option is very deep _____________, it will start acting very much like the underlying stock.

    Answer: A—In-the-money.

    Discussion: An options contract will start to move point for point with the underlying once it is very deep in-the-money. Some traders like to use deep ITM LEAPS as a proxy for buying a stock. This is because they get nearly a point move in the option for each point move in the underlying security, but the initial capital outlay is smaller.

MEDIA ASSIGNMENT

This media assignment asks the reader to calculate the deltas associated with various options. Though we can find this data on various software programs, it is good to have a basic understanding initially when looking at various option trades. Take some time to set up a few trades using the strategies already covered in this book and calculate each trade's overall position delta. Keep in mind how the delta impacts the trade. By thoroughly understanding this concept, you will be able to create winning options trades and have an easier time making additional profits by adjusting a trade back to delta neutral.

VOCABULARY DEFINITIONS

Delta: The amount by which the price of an option changes for every dollar move in the underlying instrument.

Derivatives: Derivatives are financial instruments whose value is based on the market value of an underlying asset such as a stock, bond, or commodity. Examples of derivatives are futures contracts, options, and forward contracts. Derivatives are generally used by institutional investors to increase overall portfolio return or to hedge portfolio risk.

Liquidity: The ease with which an asset can be converted to cash in the marketplace. A large number of buyers and sellers and a high volume of trading activity provide high liquidity. Liquidity is a concern for any money that may be required on short notice, whether for emergencies or for planned purchases.

Long-term equity anticipation securities (LEAPS): LEAPS are long-term stock or index options with expiration dates up to three years in the future. Like all options, they are available in two types: calls and puts.

Position delta: The sum of all positive and negative deltas in a hedged position.

Skew: A descriptive measure of lopsidedness in a distribution. It is especially important for options trading when there is volatility skew and prices are greater or less than they should be at various strikes and/or expirations.

Tick: The smallest possible movement (up or down) in the price of a security.

Volatility: The magnitude of price (or yield) changes over a predefined period of time. The amount by which an underlying instrument fluctuates in a given period of time. Options often increase in price when there is a rise in volatility even if the price of the underlying doesn't move anywhere. Volatility is a primary determinant in the valuation of options. There are two main types of volatility: historical and implied.

CHAPTER 7

The Other Greeks

SUMMARY

The option Greeks are a set of measurements that provide insight into a trade's risk exposure. This chapter reviews the four basic option Greeks—delta, gamma, theta, and vega—while analyzing their trading applications. In addition, the chapter examines how intrinsic value, time value, and volatility impact option premiums.

The Greeks help options traders minimize risk by telling us how the value of a trade will change due to fluctuations in price, time, and volatility. An option has two types of value: intrinsic and extrinsic. Intrinsic value is the real value of an option and is the amount an option is in-the-money. Intrinsic value is not affected by theta, or the passing of time. Extrinsic value, or time value, is impacted by theta. The deeper ITM an option is, the less extrinsic value the option has. An ATM or OTM option has no intrinsic value and is completely made up of extrinsic or time value. Since each option comes with an expiration date and as each day passes some time value is lost, options are called wasting assets. This is why it is important to understand theta and how it impacts an option's price over time.

Volatility has two meanings in the options field—one being historic volatility, the other implied volatility (IV). By understanding the volatility of the underlying security, we can find discrepancies in pricing. Implied volatility is a major part of an option's price, so when we see options that are showing IV that is higher than normal, we can benefit by selling the option. The same holds true for options showing low IV compared to past values, as we can buy options to benefit from a rise in IV.

QUESTIONS AND EXERCISES

1. Option Greeks are a set of measurements that explore the ____________ of a specific trade.
   A. Parameters.
   B. Delta neutral opportunities.
   C. Risk exposures.
   D. Risk-to-reward ratios.

2. Name the four basic option Greeks.
   1. ____________
   2. ____________
   3. ____________
   4. ____________

3. Fill in the option Greek term next to its appropriate definition.

Greek	Definition
________	Change in the delta of an option with respect to the change in price of its underlying security.
________	Change in the price of an option relative to the price change of the underlying security.
________	Change in the price of an option with respect to a change in its time to expiration.
________	Change in the price of an option with respect to its change in volatility.

4. The two most important components of an option's premium are ____________.
   A. Intrinsic value and extrinsic value.
   B. Vega and extrinsic value.
   C. Intrinsic value and vega.
   D. Gamma and theta.

5. For a call option, intrinsic value is equal to ____________.
   A. The strike price of the call option minus the current price of the underlying.

B. The strike price of the call option plus the current price of the underlying.

C. The current price of the underlying minus the strike price of the call option.

D. The current price of the underlying plus the strike price of the call option.

6. For a put option, intrinsic value is equal to ______________.

   A. The strike price of the put option minus the current price of the underlying.

   B. The strike price of the put option plus the current price of the underlying.

   C. The current price of the underlying minus the strike price of the put option.

   D. The current price of the underlying plus the strike price of the put option.

7. If a call or put option is out-of-the-money, the intrinsic value is equal to ______________.

   A. The strike price of the option.

   B. The price of the underlying.

   C. The price of the underlying minus the strike price of the option.

   D. Zero.

8. True or False: The intrinsic value of an option does not depend on how much time is left until expiration.

9. Time value ______________ as an option approaches expiration.

   A. Increases.

   B. Decreases.

   C. Stays the same.

10. Time value is also known as ______________.

    A. Delta.

    B. Gamma.

    C. Theta.

    D. Vega.

11. The more _____________ an option is, the less it costs.
    A. At-the-money.
    B. In-the-money.
    C. Out-of-the-money.

12. If a call option's price is less than its exercise value, investors would buy the calls and exercise them, making a guaranteed _____________ before commissions.
    A. Margin.
    B. Credit.
    C. Debit.
    D. Arbitrage profit.

13. On expiration day, all an option is worth is its _____________.
    A. Time value.
    B. Extrinsic value.
    C. Intrinsic value.
    D. Fair market value.

14. The deeper _____________ a call or put option is, the more the option moves like the underlying asset.
    A. In-the-money.
    B. Out-of-the-money.

15. Name the seven components that contribute to option pricing.
    1. ____
    2. ____
    3. ____
    4. ____
    5. ____
    6. ____
    7. ____

16. ______________ is defined as the amount by which an underlying fluctuates in a given period of time.
    A. Risk-free interest rate.
    B. Liquidity.
    C. Dividend payment.
    D. Volatility.

17. Name and describe the two main kinds of volatility.
    1. ____
       ____
    2. ____
       ____

18. Name three things understanding volatility can help you to accomplish.
    1. ____
    2. ____
    3. ____

19. ______________ is the Greek term that represents volatility.
    A. Delta.
    B. Gamma.
    C. Theta.
    D. Vega.

20. Buying options before implied volatility ______________ can cause some trades to actually end up losing money even when the price of the underlying asset moves in your direction.
    A. Rises.
    B. Drops.
    C. Stays the same for more than one week.
    D. Stays the same for more than one month.

21. When an option's actual price differs from the theoretical price by any significant amount, you can take advantage of the situation by ______________, expecting the prices to fall back in line as the expiration date approaches.
    A. Selling options with low volatility and buying options with high volatility.
    B. Selling or buying options with low volatility.
    C. Buying options with low volatility and selling options with high volatility.
    D. Buying or selling options with high volatility.

MEDIA ASSIGNMENT

The Greeks are an integral part of understanding the risk associated with various options strategies. As a result, it is important to grasp how these factors impact a trade. One of the best ways to see how the Greeks work is to experiment with an options calculator. If you have access to the Optionetics Platinum site (you can always sign up for a free two-week trial at www.optionetics.com/platinum), there is an options calculator that can be used. Or you can use the calculator available at www.cboe.com. By entering different variables for implied volatility, expiration, and strike price, we get changes in the Greeks. Seeing how the Greeks relate to each other is a great way to gain a better understanding of them and the risks associated with various options strategies.

VOCABULARY LIST

Black-Scholes option pricing model

Delta

Extrinsic value

Gamma

Historic volatility

Implied volatility

Intrinsic value

Theta

Time decay

Vega

SOLUTIONS

1. Option Greeks are a set of measurements that explore the _____________ of a specific trade.

   Answer: C—Risk exposures.

   Discussion: Each Greek encompasses various aspects of an option's risk. By understanding the Greeks you gain a better understanding of the risks of a trade. You can also make adjustments to a trade once you understand the delta dynamic. The key to successfully trading options is to maximize profits while minimizing risks. Understanding how to apply the Greeks is a prime factor in being able to accomplish this task.

2. Name the four basic option Greeks.

   Answer: Delta, gamma, theta, and vega.

   Discussion: Since each option Greek covers a specific risk, understanding each value is important to successful options trading. Delta is the most common and best-known Greek and rightfully so, but this doesn't mean the other Greeks aren't important. Depending on the type of trade entered, a different Greek might be the most important. When selling short-term options, theta is very important. If you don't want to see a sharp move in the stock, pay attention to gamma. Not only is it important to understand each Greek individually, but it also is valuable to understand how they relate to each other.

3. Fill in the option Greek term next to its appropriate definition.

   Answer:

Greek	Definition
Gamma	Change in the delta of an option with respect to the change in price of its underlying security.
Delta	Change in the price of an option relative to the price change of the underlying security
Theta	Change in the price of an option with respect to a change in its time to expiration.
Vega	Change in the price of an option with respect to its change in volatility.

   Discussion: These Greeks cover the basics of risk management for an option trade. Depending on the strategy implemented, different

Greeks might have the most impact on the trade. We often find that all the Greeks are important for certain trades, though one or the other might be the Greek that is the biggest risk to the trade. Once we understand the risks in the trade, we can make adjustments by offsetting the risks. For example, if we want to stay delta neutral and we find that a trade has become heavy on delta, we can buy puts or sell calls to adjust the delta back to zero.

4. The two most important components of an option's premium are ____________.

   Answer: A—Intrinsic value and extrinsic value.

   Discussion: Intrinsic and extrinsic value combine to make up the total value of an option. If an option is ATM or OTM it is made up completely of extrinsic (time) value. If this is the case, the option has higher theta risk. An ITM option is made up of both intrinsic and extrinsic value. However, as the option moves further ITM, its extrinsic value decreases—the more it is worth and the less time value it has. The farther OTM an option gets, the less it is worth and the more theta is a problem.

5. For a call option, intrinsic value is equal to ____________.

   Answer: C—The current price of the underlying minus the strike price of the call option.

   Discussion: A call option is ITM when the price of the underlying is above the strike price. If a call option is ITM, the intrinsic value will not be impacted by the passage of time. However, movement in the underlying will have a dramatic impact on the price of the option.

6. For a put option, intrinsic value is equal to ____________.

   Answer: A—The strike price of the put option minus the current price of the underlying.

   Discussion: A put option is ITM when the underlying is trading below the strike price. If a put option is ITM, the intrinsic value will not be impacted by the passage of time. However, movement in the underlying will have a dramatic impact on the price of the option.

7. If a call or put option is out-of-the-money, the intrinsic value is equal to ____________.

   Answer: D—Zero.

   Discussion: Both OTM and ATM options have the largest amount of time value for an option series. This means that theta will have a major impact on the price of the option going forward. ATM options normally have the most liquidity as well.

8. True or False: The intrinsic value of an option does not depend on how much time is left until expiration.

   Answer: True.

   Discussion: Only extrinsic value is affected by the passage of time. This is why it is important to understand what extrinsic and intrinsic value measure so that the proper risk management can be used. For example, you rarely want to be long options with less than 30 days until expiration. Why? Because theta has a more dramatic impact on time value during the last 30 days of an option's life.

9. Time value ______________ as an option approaches expiration.

   Answer: B—Decreases.

   Discussion: As the name infers, time has value. Thus, as time passes, its value decreases. However, time decay or theta accelerates in the last 30 days of an option's life. This is why we suggest buying options with at least 90 days until expiration so that time decay is not a major factor. We also do not normally hold long options once we have less than 30 days until expiration.

10. Time value is also known as ______________.

    Answer: C—Theta.

    Discussion: Theta is the Greek that represents time decay and time value. Theta tells us how much the option will lose each day due to time decay. If we sell an option, theta is positive. The option will increase in value due to the passage of time and the impact of time decay.

11. The more ______________ an option is, the less it costs.

    Answer: C—Out-of-the-money.

    Discussion: When an option is OTM, it has no intrinsic value and the odds of the option finishing ITM are lower. The further OTM the option gets, the less it will cost. Buying deep OTM options is a lot like buying a lottery ticket. If an option is several strikes OTM, it might have a delta of 10 to 15, which means there is only a 10 to 15 percent chance the option will finish in-the-money by expiration.

12. If a call option's price is less than its intrinsic value, investors would buy the calls and exercise them, making a guaranteed ______________ before commissions.

    Answer: D—Arbitrage profit.

    Discussion: This occurs very infrequently, but it is important to understand the concept. If the call option we hold is trading for less than the intrinsic value of the option, we are better off exercising the option and taking the guaranteed profits. If an option is trading for $4.95, but is $5.00 ITM, we could exercise the option and pocket the $0.05 difference.

13. On expiration day, all an option is worth is its ____________.

    Answer: C—Intrinsic value.

    Discussion: This should make sense because when time is up, all that is left is actual value or intrinsic value. An option that is OTM will see a sharp decrease in value as expiration day approaches.

14. The deeper ____________ a call or put option is, the more the option moves like the underlying asset.

    Answer: A—In-the-money.

    Discussion: As an option moves deeper ITM, its delta increases and this means the option starts to move more like the underlying security. For example, a deep ITM call might have a delta of 90, which means that for every dollar move in the underlying, the option will increase by $0.90.

15. Name the seven components that contribute to option pricing.

    Answer:

    1. The current price of the underlying financial instrument.
    2. The strike price of the option.
    3. The type of option (put or call).
    4. The amount of time remaining until expiration.
    5. The current risk-free interest rate.
    6. The volatility of the underlying financial instrument.
    7. The dividend rate, if any, of the underlying financial instrument.

    Discussion: All seven of these components have an impact on an option's price. Some have a larger impact than others. We didn't discuss how interest rates and dividends affect option prices because their effects are minimal as compared with the other five. Using an options calculator, a trader can identify the values for the different Greeks.

16. ____________ is defined as the amount by which an underlying fluctuates in a given period of time.

    Answer: D—Volatility.

    Discussion: Volatility is an important component in trading options. Many traders see volatility as a negative, but used the right way, volatility is a great tool for making profits. However, we need to understand what is meant by volatility and the different meanings that it has.

17. Name and describe the two main kinds of volatility.

Answer:

1. Historical volatility gauges price movement in terms of past performance and is calculated by using the standard deviation of the underlying asset's price changes from close-to-close of trading going back 21 to 23 days (or any predetermined time frame).
2. Implied volatility approximates how much the marketplace thinks prices will move and is calculated by using an option pricing model (Black-Scholes for stocks and indexes and Black for futures).

Discussion: Historical volatility is the past and though this doesn't have an impact on the future, it can be a guide to how the stock might be expected to trade. Implied volatility, calculated using an option pricing model, is the volatility that is expected in the future. Much of the time, historic and implied volatility run close together, but there are times when they differ and these divergences are good times to utilize various option strategies.

18. Name three things understanding volatility can help you to accomplish.

Answer:

1. Helps you to choose and implement the appropriate option strategy.
2. Holds the key to improving your market timing.
3. Helps you to avoid the purchase of overpriced options or the sale of underpriced options.

Discussion: All three of these factors are very important, as they all help options traders limit risk and maximize profits. By knowing when implied volatility is high, we can avoid buying overpriced options and concentrate on selling them. When IV is low, going long options is often a good strategy, while selling options isn't. There are various option strategies that take advantage of the different levels of IV.

19. ______________ is the Greek term that represents volatility.

Answer: D—Vega.

Discussion: Vega tells us how much an option's price will change for a percentage change in IV. A change in IV can have a major impact on an option's price, so it is important to understand how vega impacts a trade. IV can rise sharply even without movement in the underlying security, so it is important to know how the option will be affected by this change in IV. This is what vega tells us.

20. Buying options before implied volatility ____________ can cause some trades to actually end up losing money even when the price of the underlying asset moves in your direction.

    Answer: B—Drops.

    Discussion: This is called a volatility crush and it is discouraging when it happens. It is frustrating to be right about direction, but see your option gain nothing or actually lose money. This often happens when a pending news announcement is released such as earnings or a Food and Drug Administration (FDA) decision. The idea is that IV rises ahead of the report, but drops sharply once the news is actually out. This is why we do not normally want to buy options that are showing relatively high IV.

21. When an option's actual price differs from the theoretical price by any significant amount, you can take advantage of the situation by ____________, expecting the prices to fall back in line as the expiration date approaches.

    Answer: C—Buying options with low volatility and selling options with high volatility.

    Discussion: Implied volatility is like elastic, stretching to extremes but normally coming back to an average level. This is called mean reversion and it allows options traders to take advantage of situations when the actual price varies from the theoretical price.

MEDIA ASSIGNMENT

The mathematics of options can be rather complicated, but the use of an options calculator is important to a trader's success. We need to know only a few different variables and we can calculate the Greeks as well as the implied volatility of a stock. Experimenting with an options calculator should provide some insight to how the Greeks change in relation to various changes in other Greeks or movement by the underlying security.

VOCABULARY DEFINITIONS

Black-Scholes option pricing model: A model used to calculate option pricing based on a variety of factors including: the risk-free interest rate, the standard deviation of the underlying stock, time left until expiration, and the exercise (strike) price.

Delta: The amount by which the price of an option changes for every dollar move in the underlying instrument.

Extrinsic value: The price of an option less its intrinsic value. An at-the-money or out-of-the-money option's worth consists of nothing but extrinsic or time value.

Gamma: The degree by which the delta changes with respect to changes in the underlying instrument's price.

Historic volatility: A measurement of how much a contract's price has fluctuated over a period of time in the past; usually calculated by taking a standard deviation of price changes over a specific time period.

Implied volatility: Volatility computed using the actual market price of an option and a pricing model (Black-Scholes). For example, if the market price of an option rises without a change in the price of the underlying stock or future, implied volatility will have risen.

Intrinsic value: The amount by which a market is in-the-money. At-the-money and out-of-the-money options have no intrinsic value. Call Intrinsic value = underlying – strike price. Put Intrinsic value = strike price – underlying.

Theta: The ratio of the change in an option's price to the decrease in its time to expiration.

Time decay: The amount of value lost in an option due to the passage of time.

Vega: The amount by which the price of an option changes when the volatility changes.

CHAPTER 8

Straddles, Strangles, and Synthetics

SUMMARY

This chapter reviews several delta neutral strategies including straddles, strangles, and synthetic straddles. These strategies are based on optimal mathematical relationships and have a high probability of profitability if applied in suitable markets. Examples of each strategy are included to enable the reader to become fully acquainted with the calculations of risk, reward, and breakevens. This chapter covers both limited risk and unlimited risk strategies (short straddles and short strangles). Keep in mind that I do not recommend placing unlimited risk strategies; they are included so that readers are introduced to the mechanics involved.

A long straddle and strangle form a U-shaped risk graph, which visually conveys the unlimited reward and limited risk nature of these delta neutral strategies. This type of risk graph is also available when trading a long synthetic straddle with calls or puts. Short straddles and strangles have an upside-down U-shaped risk graph, which tells us that the reward is limited and the risk is unlimited.

Straddles, strangles, and synthetic straddles are all delta neutral strategies to start. Synthetic straddles can be adjusted over time, which makes them a favorite for many traders. New traders often do not understand how simultaneously buying a put and a call can be profitable. The idea is that as a stock moves, one side of the straddle or strangle will see a larger gain than the other side will see a loss. If the underlying asset rises in price, the losing option can only fall to zero, whereas the profitable option can rise indefinitely.

As with any strategy, a trader should view a risk graph before entering a trade. By finding stocks that have been consolidating but have impending news, a trader can see nice, relatively safer profits using straddles, strangles, and synthetic straddles.

QUESTIONS AND EXERCISES

1. Setting up a delta neutral trade requires selecting a calculated ratio of short and long positions to create an overall position delta of ______________.
   A. +100.
   B. –100.
   C. +50.
   D. Zero.

2. The delta of 100 shares of stock or one futures contract equals plus or minus ______________.
   A. 500.
   B. 100.
   C. 50.
   D. Zero.

3. The delta of an option depends on its ______________.
   A. Expiration date.
   B. Volatility.
   C. Strike price.
   D. Premium.

4. Name two ways of creating a delta neutral trade with ATM options if you are buying 100 shares of stock.
   1. ____
   2. ____

5. Name two ways of creating a delta neutral trade with ATM options if you are selling 100 shares of stock.
   1. ____
   2. ____

6. By purchasing futures and buying puts, a U-shaped risk graph is created that reflects ______________.
   A. Limited profit potential with limited risk.
   B. Limited profit potential with unlimited risk.
   C. Unlimited profit potential with unlimited risk.
   D. Unlimited profit potential with limited risk.

7. By purchasing stock and selling calls, an upside-down U-shaped risk graph is created that reflects the trade's ______________.
   A. Limited profit potential with limited risk.
   B. Limited profit potential with unlimited risk.
   C. Unlimited profit potential with unlimited risk.
   D. Unlimited profit potential with limited risk.

8. By selling 100 XYZ shares and buying 2 ATM calls, what kind of risk curve are you creating?
   A. U-shaped risk curve with unlimited profit potential and limited risk.
   B. U-shaped risk curve with limited profit potential and unlimited risk.
   C. Upside-down U-shaped risk curve with unlimited profit potential and limited risk.
   D. Upside-down U-shaped risk curve with limited profit potential and unlimited risk.

9. By selling 100 XYZ shares and selling two ATM puts, what kind of risk curve are you creating?
   A. U-shaped risk curve with unlimited profit potential and limited risk.
   B. U-shaped risk curve with limited profit potential and unlimited risk.
   C. Upside-down U-shaped risk curve with unlimited profit potential and limited risk.
   D. Upside-down U-shaped risk curve with limited profit potential and unlimited risk.

10. Buying a straddle involves buying both a call and a put with ______________.
    A. Different strike prices and identical expiration months.
    B. Identical strike prices and different expiration months.
    C. Identical strike prices and expiration months.
    D. Different strike prices and expiration months.

11. To place a long straddle, it is optimal to locate a market with ______________.
    - A. High volatility expecting a volatility decrease.
    - B. Low volatility expecting a volatility increase.
    - C. Continuous high liquidity.
    - D. Continuous low liquidity.

12. Long straddles create what kind of risk profiles?
    - A. V-shaped risk curves with unlimited profit potential and limited risk.
    - B. V-shaped risk curves with limited profit potential and unlimited risk.
    - C. Upside-down V-shaped risk curves with unlimited profit potential and limited risk.
    - D. Upside-down V-shaped risk curves with limited profit potential and unlimited risk.

13. How is the upside breakeven of a long straddle calculated?

    ____

14. How is the downside breakeven of a long straddle calculated?

    ____

15. Calculate the values for the following long straddle:

    Long 1 November ATM DELL 35 Call @ 2.45

    Long 1 November ATM DELL 35 Put @ 2.20

    DELL is currently trading at $35.10.

    Put cost = ______________________________

    Call cost = ______________________________

    Maximum reward = ______________________________

    Maximum risk = ______________________________

    Upside breakeven = ______________________________

    Downside breakeven = ______________________________

    Range of profitability = ______________________________

16. Short straddles create what kind of risk profiles?
    A. V-shaped risk curves with unlimited profit potential and limited risk.
    B. V-shaped risk curves with limited profit potential and unlimited risk.
    C. Upside-down V-shaped risk curves with unlimited profit potential and limited risk.
    D. Upside-down V-shaped risk curves with limited profit potential and unlimited risk.

17. Calculate the values for the following short straddle:

    Short 1 July SMH 37.50 Call @ 1.50

    Short 1 July SMH 37.50 Put @ 1.25

    SMH is trading at $37.71.

    Put credit = ______________________

    Call credit = ______________________

    Maximum reward = ______________________

    Maximum risk = ______________________

    Upside breakeven = ______________________

    Downside breakeven = ______________________

    Range of profitability = ______________________

18. Strangles are quite similar to straddles, except ____________.
    A. The options have different expiration months.
    B. One option is short and the other is long.
    C. The options are ITM instead of ATM.
    D. The options are OTM instead of ATM.

19. Long strangles involve buying both an OTM call and an OTM put with ____________.
    A. Different strike prices and identical expiration months.
    B. Identical strike prices and different expiration months.
    C. Identical strike prices and expiration months.
    D. Different strike prices and expiration months.

20. A long strangle has ________________________________.
    A. Limited profit potential and limited risk.
    B. Limited profit potential and unlimited risk.
    C. Unlimited profit potential and unlimited risk.
    D. Unlimited profit potential and limited risk.

21. Calculate the values for the following long strangle example:

    Long 1 November DELL 40 Call @ 0.65

    Long 1 November DELL 30 Put @ 0.70

    DELL is currently trading at $35.10.

    Put cost = ________________________________

    Call cost = ________________________________

    Maximum reward = ________________________________

    Maximum risk = ________________________________

    Upside breakeven = ________________________________

    Downside breakeven = ________________________________

    Range of profitability = ________________________________

22. True or False: Fixed straddles can be adjusted as the market moves back and forth.

23. Name two ways of creating a long synthetic straddle using a stock.

    1. ________________________________
    2. ________________________________

24. Calculate the values for the following long synthetic straddle example:

    Long 100 Shares of DELL @ $35.10

    Long 2 November DELL 35 Puts @ 2.20

    Stock cost = ________________________________

    Put cost = ________________________________

Maximum reward = ______________________________

Maximum risk = ______________________________

Upside breakeven = ______________________________

Downside breakeven = ______________________________

Range of profitability = ______________________________

25. Calculate the values for the following long synthetic straddle example:

    Short 100 Shares of DELL @ $35.10

    Long 2 November DELL 35 Calls @ 6.85

    Stock cost = ______________________________

    Call cost = ______________________________

    Maximum reward = ______________________________

    Maximum risk = ______________________________

    Upside breakeven = ______________________________

    Downside breakeven = ______________________________

    Range of profitability = ______________________________

MEDIA ASSIGNMENT

Delta neutral strategies take away the necessity to predict market direction. However, we still need to find stocks that are expected to show volatility and to choose options with low implied volatility. For this media assignment, identify several securities that are good candidates for delta neutral strategies. Before entering the data into the Optionetics Platinum site, take the time to manually calculate the details of the trade, including the breakeven points, maximum risk and profit, and the range of profitability. After you have calculated this data, plug it into Optionetics Platinum (or some other options program) and see if your calculations are correct. As an added bonus, check out the risk graphs as well. Compare the risk graphs for various strategies, including straddles, strangles, and long synthetic straddles.

VOCABULARY LIST

Average Directional Movement Index (ADX)

Delta

Delta neutral trade

Long straddle

Long strangle

Long synthetic straddle

Risk graph

Straddle

Strangle

SOLUTIONS

1. Setting up a delta neutral trade requires selecting a calculated ratio of short and long positions to create an overall position delta of ______________.

   Answer: D—Zero.

   Discussion: The idea with a delta neutral trade is to get the overall delta as close to zero as possible. Of course, there will be trades that have slightly positive or negative deltas, but this doesn't mean they won't have a similar risk graph to a perfectly delta neutral trade.

2. The delta of 100 shares of stock or one futures contract equals plus or minus ______________.

   Answer: B—100.

   Discussion: Unlike options, futures and stocks do not have fractional deltas. They have deltas equal to 1.00. This allows a trader to set up strategies that incorporate options, stock, and/or futures to create delta neutral strategies. Obviously, if we buy 100 shares of stock and sell 100 shares of the same stock, there is no way to make a profit. However, by creating synthetic positions, we can make a profit using options without needing to predict market direction.

3. The delta of an option depends on its ______________.

   Answer: C—Strike price.

   Discussion: One definition of delta is that it tells the trader the odds of an option finishing in-the-money by expiration. Thus, the farther away the option strike is from the stock price (in the unprofitable direction), the lower the delta. In-the-money options have deltas generally above 50, while out-of-the-money options have deltas below 50.

4. Name two ways of creating a delta neutral trade with ATM options if you are buying 100 shares of stock.

   Answer: Buy two ATM puts or sell two ATM calls.

   Discussion: One hundred shares of stock equals +100 deltas, so we need to create a combination of options that equal –100 deltas. The easiest way to create –100 deltas is to sell two ATM calls or to buy two ATM puts. Though the delta might not be exactly –100, using ATM options will make the delta close enough to this figure.

5. Name two ways of creating a delta neutral trade with ATM options if you are selling 100 shares of stock.

   Answer: Buy two ATM calls or sell two ATM puts.

   Discussion: To offset –100 deltas that comes from selling the stock, you can buy two ATM calls or sell two ATM puts to bring in +100 delta. The idea is that anything bullish creates a positive delta and anything bearish creates a negative delta.

6. By purchasing futures and buying puts, a U-shaped risk graph is created that reflects ______________.

   Answer: D—Unlimited profit potential with limited risk.

   Discussion: This is the optimal type of risk graph delta neutral traders like to see. Though not all options strategies are created with unlimited reward and limited risk, this is what we strive to achieve.

7. By purchasing stock and selling calls, an upside-down U-shaped risk graph is created that reflects the trade's ______________.

   Answer: B—Limited profit potential with unlimited risk.

   Discussion: An upside-down U is exactly the opposite of what delta neutral traders want to see, as it shows unlimited risk and limited profits. Though this type of trade might be profitable most of the time, it takes only one trade that goes wrong to erase an entire trading account.

8. By selling 100 XYZ shares and buying two ATM calls, what kind of risk curve are you creating?

   Answer: A—U-shaped risk curve with unlimited profit potential and limited risk.

Discussion: This position is called a long synthetic straddle using calls. The U shape is created because the trade profits on a sharp move lower or a sharp move higher. If the stock stays flat, then a loss would most likely be incurred.

9. By selling 100 XYZ shares and selling two ATM puts, what kind of risk curve are you creating?

   Answer: D—Upside-down U-shaped risk curve with limited profit potential and unlimited risk.

   Discussion: This trade is a short synthetic straddle using puts. By selling both the stock and the puts, the maximum profit is the credit received from selling the puts and stock. However, if the underlying moves sharply in either direction, a large loss can be incurred.

10. Buying a straddle involves buying both a call and a put with ______________.

    Answer: C—Identical strike prices and expiration months.

    Discussion: Composed of both a long ATM call and a long ATM put, a straddle makes money when the underlying asset moves sharply in either direction. As the stock moves higher, the call increases in value faster than the put loses money. The opposite also holds true, with a decline in the stock's price increasing the value of the put faster than the loss incurred in the call.

11. To place a long straddle, it is optimal to locate a market with ______________.

    Answer: B—Low volatility expecting a volatility increase.

    Discussion: A long straddle consists of buying two options. Implied volatility has a major impact on the price of an option, so we want to buy options that have historically low IV. This puts the odds of success higher for a straddle trader. Straddle traders also want to see a volatility increase because this means a larger move in the underlying security.

12. Long straddles create what kind of risk profiles?

    Answer: A—V-shaped risk curves with unlimited profit potential and limited risk.

    Discussion: Just like a long synthetic straddle, a straddle has unlimited profit potential and limited risk. This is what we are looking for when we enter a delta neutral trade.

13. How is the upside breakeven of a long straddle calculated?

    Answer: Upside breakeven = strike price + net debit.

    Discussion: The upside breakeven at expiration is calculated by adding the net debit required to enter the trade to the strike price. However, this doesn't mean that a profit can't be made before expiration on a smaller move if volatility increases in magnitude.

14. How is the downside breakeven of a long straddle calculated?

    Answer: Downside breakeven = strike price – net debit.

    Discussion: The downside breakeven at expiration is calculated by subtracting the net debit required to enter the trade from the strike price. However, this doesn't mean that a profit can't be made before expiration on a smaller move if volatility increases in magnitude. You will rarely hold a straddle until expiration, anyway.

15. Calculate the values for the following long straddle:

    Long 1 November ATM DELL 35 Call @ 2.45

    Long 1 November ATM DELL 35 Put @ 2.20

    DELL is currently trading at $35.10.

    Answer:

    Put cost = 2.20 or $220.

    Call cost = 2.45 or $245.

    Maximum reward = Unlimited to the upside and limited to the downside (as the underlying can only fall to zero) beyond the breakevens.

    Maximum risk = (2.45 + 2.20) × 100 = $465 (Total debit).

    Upside breakeven = (35 + 4.65) = $39.65 (Call strike + net debit).

    Downside breakeven = (35 – 4.65) = $30.35 (Put strike – net debit).

    Range of profitability = Above $39.65 and below $30.35.

    Discussion: The breakeven points, maximum risk and reward, and total costs are important values to understand before entering a trade. These values can be figured manually, or you can use a program like Optionetics Platinum to calculate these details. Either way, it is very important to assess a trade's risks before jumping in and putting real money on the line.

16. Short straddles create what kind of risk profiles?

    Answer: D—Upside-down V-shaped risk curves with limited profit potential and unlimited risk.

Discussion: A short straddle or strangle creates an upside-down V-shaped risk graph. This is not the kind of risk profile that a delta neutral trader wants to see. Though this type of trade might have a high winning percentage in sideways-moving markets, it takes only one sharp move to wipe out a trading account.

17. Calculate the values for the following short straddle:

    Short 1 July SMH 37.50 Call @ 1.50

    Short 1 July SMH 37.50 Put @ 1.25

    SMH is trading at $37.71.

    Answer:

    Put credit = 1.25 or $125.

    Call credit = 1.50 or $150.

    Maximum reward = $(1.25 + 1.50) \times 100$ = $275 (Limited to the net credit).

    Maximum risk = Unlimited to the upside and limited to the downside (as the underlying can only fall to zero) beyond the breakevens.

    Upside breakeven = (37.50 + 2.75) = $40.25 (ATM strike price + net credit).

    Downside breakeven = (37.50 – 2.75) = $34.75 (ATM strike price – net credit).

    Range of profitability = Between $34.75 and $40.25.

18. Strangles are quite similar to straddles, except ______________.

    Answer: D—The options are OTM instead of ATM.

    Discussion: Strangles have a similar risk profile to a straddle, except that the maximum loss area is wider. However, the initial cost to enter a strangle is lower. Keep in mind that the underlying asset has to make a larger move for the trade to become profitable.

19. Long strangles involve buying both an OTM call and an OTM put with ______________

    Answer: A—Different strike prices and identical expiration months.

    Discussion: By using OTM options, the trader's cost to enter a strangle is less than the cost to enter a straddle. However, because the options are OTM, the underlying security has to see a larger move to garner a profit.

20. A long strangle has ______________.

    Answer: D—Unlimited profit potential and limited risk.

    Discussion: Just like a straddle, a strangle has limited risk and unlimited profit potential. The main difference is that there is a wider area between the two strike prices where the maximum loss is incurred. Whether to use a straddle or a strangle is a personal decision and should be based on the outlook for the stock and the risk graph.

21. Calculate the values for the following long strangle example:

    Long 1 November DELL 40 Call @ 0.65

    Long 1 November DELL 30 Put @ 0.70

    DELL is currently trading at $35.10.

    Answer:

    Put cost = 0.70 or $70.

    Call cost = 0.65 or $65.

    Maximum reward = Unlimited to the upside and downside beyond the breakevens.

    Maximum risk = (.70 + .65) × 100 = $135 (Total debit).

    Upside breakeven = (40 + 1.35) = $41.35 (Call strike + net debit).

    Downside breakeven = (30 – 1.35) = $28.65 (Put strike – net debit).

    Range of profitability = Above $41.35 and below $28.65.

    Discussion: The cost to enter a strangle is lower than the cost of a straddle. However, by comparing the straddle and strangle example, we can see that a strangle takes a much larger move to break even and make a profit. The maximum risk area is also much larger, falling between the two breakevens. A straddle sees a maximum loss only if the underlying closes right on the ATM strike price.

22. True or False: Fixed straddles can be adjusted as the market moves back and forth.

    Answer: False.

    Discussion: Fixed straddles cannot be adjusted. If you want to be able to make adjustments as the trade progresses, then look at using long synthetic straddles.

23. Name two ways of creating a long synthetic straddle using a stock.

    Answer:

    1. Sell 100 shares and buy two ATM calls.
    2. Buy 100 shares and buy two ATM puts.

Discussion: A long synthetic straddle is a delta neutral trade that consists of shares of stock against long options. A long synthetic straddle with multiple contracts can be adjusted back to delta neutral as the trade progresses. The risk profile is similar to a straddle but has a U-shaped risk curve instead of a V-shaped one. A trader doesn't need to use ATM options, but this is the easiest way to create a long synthetic straddle.

24. Calculate the values for the following long synthetic straddle example:

    Long 100 Shares of DELL @ $35.10

    Long 2 November DELL 35 Puts @ 2.20

    Answer:

    Maximum reward = Unlimited.

    Maximum risk = [(2 × 2.20) + (35.10 – 35)] × 100 = $450 {Net debit of options + [(Price of underlying stock at initiation – option strike price) × number of shares]}.

    Upside breakeven = (35.10 + 4.40) = $39.50 (Price of underlying stock at initiation + net debit of options).

    Downside breakeven = [(2 × 35) – 35.10] – 4.40 = $30.50 {[(2 × option strike) – price of underlying stock at initiation] – net debit of options}.

    Range of profitability = Above $39.50 and below $30.50.

    Discussion: The breakeven points take a little more calculating because the stock price isn't exactly at $35. Though this calculation can still be made manually, it is much easier to use a program like Optionetics Platinum.

25. Calculate the values for the following long synthetic straddle example:

    Short 100 Shares of DELL @ $35.10

    Long 2 November DELL 35 Calls @ 6.85

    Answer:

    Maximum reward = Unlimited.

    Maximum risk = [(2 × 6.85) + (35 – 35.10)] × 100 = $1,360 {[Net debit of options + (option strike – price of underlying at initiation)] × number of shares.

    Upside breakeven = [(2 × 35) – 35.10] + 13.70) = $48.60 {[(2 × option strike) – price of underlying stock at initiation] + net debit of options}.

Downside breakeven = 35.10 – 13.70 = $21.40 (Price of underlying stock at initiation – net debit of options).

Range of profitability = Below $21.40 and above $48.60.

Discussion: By comparing the risk graphs and different variables, a trader can decide whether to short shares and buy calls or to buy shares and buy puts to create a long synthetic straddle. Ultimately, we want to enter the trade that provides the best reward-to-risk ratio.

MEDIA ASSIGNMENT

Although there are computer programs that will generate risk graphs and the details of a particular options strategy, it is very helpful to understand how these details are figured manually. In doing this media assignment, not only should you gain a better understanding of the risks of a trade, but you'll appreciate how a computer speeds up the process.

VOCABULARY DEFINITIONS

Average Directional Movement Index (ADX): An indicator developed by J. Welles Wilder to measure market trend intensity. It does not give signals regarding direction, but tells traders whether the stock or index is in the midst of a healthy trend (either up or down). The idea is for directional traders to stay out of choppy or sideways markets (i.e., when the stock or index is not trending), and commit to the markets only when the stock or index is moving within a clear trend.

Delta: The amount by which the price of an option changes for every dollar move in the underlying instrument.

Delta neutral trade: This is an options/options or options/underlying instrument position constructed so that it is relatively insensitive to the price movement of the underlying instruments. This is arranged by selecting a calculated ratio of short and long positions with a combined position delta of zero.

Long straddle: A non-directional option strategy that combines the simultaneous purchase of the same number of ATM puts and calls with identical expirations. The maximum loss is limited to the net debit of the options. The upside breakeven is equal to the net debit plus the strike price, and the downside breakeven is calculated by subtracting the net debit from the strike price. The maximum profit is unlimited to the upside and limited to the downside (as the underlying can only fall to zero) beyond the breakevens.

Long strangle: The purchase of an OTM call and an OTM put with the same expiration date. Look for a stable market where you anticipate a large volatility spike. The maximum risk is limited to the net debit paid. The maximum profit is unlimited to the upside and limited to the downside (as the underlying can only fall to zero) beyond the breakevens. The upside breakeven is calculated by adding the call strike to the net debit, and the downside breakeven is calculated by subtracting the net debit from the put strike.

Long synthetic straddle: A delta neutral trade in which two long options are balanced out by 100 shares of stock. Look for a market with low volatility where you anticipate a volatility increase resulting in stock price movement in either direction beyond the breakevens.

Risk graph: A graphical representation of risk and reward on any given trade.

Straddle: A position consisting of a long (or short) call and a long (or short) put, where both options have the same strike price and expiration date.

Strangle: A position that consists of a long (or short) OTM call and a long (or short) OTM put where both options have the same underlying and same expiration date, but different strike prices.

CHAPTER 9

Advanced Delta Neutral Strategies

SUMMARY

Most successful options traders are continuously accessing risk-reward probabilities. Trades that offer limited rewards but high risks are often ill-advised. Instead, experienced strategists tend to focus on situations that offer high rewards and limited risks. In order to find these more attractive scenarios, traders work to develop more complex strategies and study the probabilities of success or failure using risk graphs.

In this chapter, the reader is introduced to four advanced delta neutral strategies: ratio call spreads, ratio put spreads, call ratio backspreads and put ratio backspreads. These strategies are a bit more complex and involve simultaneously buying and selling either puts or calls in different quantities. For example, ratio spreads involve either all puts or all calls and are established by purchasing a put or call and selling a greater number of puts or calls. Ratio spreads provide a wide profit zone, but come with unlimited risk. Ratio backspreads, on the other hand, involve selling one or more options (puts or calls) and buying a greater number of options (puts or calls). Ratio backspreads are generally initiated as credit trades and offer limited risk with unlimited reward potential, which is the optional type of situation for experienced options traders.

QUESTIONS AND EXERCISES

1. A ratio spread is a strategy in which an _____________ number of option contracts of the same underlying instrument are bought and sold.

A. Even.

B. Uneven.

2. A ratio call spread involves ______________.

A. Buying a lower strike option and selling a greater number of ITM options.

B. Buying a higher strike option and selling a greater number of ATM options.

C. Buying a lower strike option and selling a greater number of OTM options.

D. Buying a higher strike option and selling a greater number of OTM options.

3. Calculate the values for the following ratio call spread:

Long 1 January QQQ 37 Call @ 2.50

Short 2 January QQQ 40 Calls @ 1.50

Net credit = ______________________________

Maximum reward = ______________________________

Maximum risk = ______________________________

Upside breakeven = ______________________________

4. A ratio call spread should be implemented in a/an ______________ market.

A. Bullish.

B. Bearish.

C. Either bullish or bearish.

5. A ratio put spread involves ______________.

A. Buying a higher strike put option and selling a greater number of OTM put options.

B. Buying a lower strike put option and selling a greater number of OTM put options.

C. Buying a higher strike put option and selling a greater number of ITM put options.

D. Buying a lower strike put option and selling a greater number of ITM put options.

6. Calculate the values for the following ratio put spread:

   Long 1 January QQQ 35 Put @ 2.00

   Short 2 January QQQ 32 Puts @ 1.25

   Net credit = ______________________________

   Maximum profit = ______________________________

   Maximum risk = ______________________________

   Downside breakeven = ______________________________

7. A ratio put spread should be implemented in a/an ____________ market.
   - A. Bullish.
   - B. Bearish.
   - C. Either bullish or bearish.

8. True or False: Never attempt to place a ratio backspread in a market with low volatility.

9. A call ratio backspread involves ____________.
   - A. Selling a higher strike call and buying a greater number of lower strike calls.
   - B. Selling a lower strike call and buying a greater number of higher strike calls.
   - C. Buying a higher strike call and selling a greater number of lower strike calls.
   - D. Buying a lower strike call and selling a greater number of higher strike calls.

10. Calculate the values for the following call ratio backspread:

    Short 2 January QQQ 35 Calls @ 4.00

    Long 3 January QQQ 38 Calls @ 2.25

    Net credit = ______________________________

    Maximum profit = ______________________________

    Maximum risk = ______________________________

    Upside breakeven = ______________________________

    Downside breakeven = ______________________________

11. Call ratio backspreads are best implemented during periods of ____________.

    A. High volatility in a highly volatile market that shows signs of increasing activity to the upside.
    B. High volatility in a highly volatile market that shows signs of increasing activity to the downside.
    C. Low volatility in a highly volatile market that shows signs of increasing activity to the upside.
    D. Low volatility in a highly volatile market that shows signs of increasing activity to the downside.

12. Put ratio backspreads are best implemented during periods of ____________.

    A. High volatility in a highly volatile market that shows signs of increasing activity to the upside.
    B. High volatility in a highly volatile market that shows signs of increasing activity to the downside.
    C. Low volatility in a highly volatile market that shows signs of increasing activity to the upside.
    D. Low volatility in a highly volatile market that shows signs of increasing activity to the downside.

13. A put ratio backspread involves ____________.

    A. Selling a higher strike put and buying a greater number of lower strike puts.
    B. Selling a lower strike put and buying a greater number of higher strike puts.
    C. Buying a higher strike put and selling a greater number of lower strike puts.
    D. Buying a lower strike put and selling a greater number of higher strike puts.

14. Calculate the values for the following put ratio backspread:

    Short 2 January QQQ 35 Puts @ 2.50

    Long 3 January QQQ 32 Puts @ 1.25

    Net credit/debit = ____________________________________

    Maximum profit = ____________________________________

Maximum risk = ______________________________

Upside breakeven = ______________________________

Downside breakeven = ______________________________

15. What is the difference between a forward and a reverse volatility skew?

____

____

MEDIA ASSIGNMENT

In Chapter 4, the media assignment used the free options calculator from the Chicago Board Options Exchange web site at www.cboe.com to create a risk curve for the long call. Let's go back to that calculator and repeat the process using a more complex strategy. So, from the CBOE home page, click on the "Trading Tools" tab and then the "Volatility Optimizer" and then click on "Options Calculator." Next, select "American" in the style box. (*Note:* If, for some reason the CBOE site is not available, readers can use any online options calculator to complete this assignment.)

Start by creating a table with the following column heads: stock price, long call price, value of two long calls, value of short call, and overall position value. Then, on a piece of graph paper (or using a Microsoft Excel printout), create a risk graph by drawing a horizontal axis and a vertical axis. Along the horizontal axis, write the numbers 60, 65, 70, 75, 80, 85, and 90 at evenly spaced intervals. From bottom to top, write the numbers –5, –4, –3, –2, –1, 0, 1, 2, 3, 4, 5, 6, 7, 8, 9, and 10 along the vertical axis.

Using the chart and the options calculator, let's create a risk curve for a call ratio backspread. In this example, the call ratio backspread involves selling an at-the-money call option and buying two out-of-the-money options. Let's use the strike prices of 65 and 75.

Now input some variables into the calculator regarding the long calls. First, let the strike price equal 75; the volatility is 30 percent, the annual interest rate is 5 percent, and the company pays no dividend (quarterly dividend amount equals 0). Next, in the "Days Left to Expiration" box, click "Days Until Expiration" and enter the number 100. We are going to buy two long calls that have 100 days remaining until expiration, a strike price of 75, volatility of 30 percent, and an underlying security that pays no dividends. At the same time, we will sell short one call with a strike price of 65, 100 days left until expiration, and volatility of 30 percent.

Now, let's look at the position as the stock price changes. Enter 60 into the "Equity Price" box and look at the value of the long call. It has a value of 45 cents. Since there are two long calls in this trade, the total value of the long calls is 90 cents. Now, the short call is worth $2.20. So, the value of the position is –$1.30. Put a dot on the risk graph where the position value equals –$130 and the stock price equals 60. Now, repeat the calculation for the stock prices 70 through 90. When you reach the final equity price value of 90, the long call is worth roughly $1,650 a contract and the two long calls equal $3,300. The short call is worth $2,600 a contract. Subtract the value of the short call from the long calls and the call ratio backspread is worth $7. Finally, connect the dots and you have just created a risk curve for this trade. It is U-shaped, but also upward sloping to the right. (*Note:* In practice, the risk curve will look a bit different than the one drawn in this example because we have not factored in the credit received or premium paid for the trade. Nevertheless, the risk curve of any call ratio backspread will take on a shape similar to the one drawn here.)

VOCABULARY LIST

Call ratio backspread
Forward volatility skew
Nondirectional
Price skew
Put ratio backspread
Ratio backspread
Ratio call spread
Ratio put spread
Ratio spread
Reverse volatility skew
Time skew
Volatility skew

SOLUTIONS

1. A ratio spread is a strategy in which an ____________ number of option contracts of the same underlying instrument are bought and sold.

   Answer: B—Uneven.

   Discussion: To create a ratio spread, the strategist will sell one or more at-the-money or near-the-money options and sell a greater number of out-of-the-money contracts. The trade can be created using either puts or calls.

2. A ratio call spread involves ______________.

   Answer: C—Buying a lower strike option and selling a greater number of OTM options.

   Discussion: As the name implies, the ratio call spread is established with call options. The strategist will buy one or more calls and sell a greater number of calls with a higher strike price. Common ratios include 1-to-2 and 2-to-3.

3. Calculate the values for the following ratio call spread:

   Long 1 January QQQ 37 Call @ 2.50

   Short 2 January QQQ 40 Calls @ 1.50

   Answer:

   Net credit = $[(2 \times 1.50) - 2.50] \times 100 = \$50$ [(Short – long premium) × 100].

   Maximum reward = $[1 \times (40 - 37) + .50] \times 100 = \$350$ [Number of long contracts × (difference in strikes + net credit)] × 100.

   Maximum risk = Unlimited to the upside above the breakeven.

   Upside breakeven = $37 + [(40 - 37) \times 2 \div (2 - 1)] + .50 = \$43.50$ {Lower strike + [(difference in strikes × number of short contracts) ÷ (number of short calls – number of long calls)] + net credit}.

   Discussion: The credit received for the ratio call spread equals the premium received from the sale of the calls minus the premium paid for the purchase of the call(s) with the lower strike price(s). In this case, it equals $3.00 minus $2.50, or $50 per contract. The maximum reward occurs if both short calls expire worthless and the long call is closed at or near expiration for a profit. In this case, the premium kept from the long calls if the QQQ reaches exactly $40 equals $300. At that point, the long call yields a $50 profit and the maximum gain is therefore $350.

4. A ratio call spread should be implemented in a/an ______________ market.

   Answer: B—Bearish.

   Discussion: The ratio call spread is best established when the strategist expects the underlying asset to move only modestly higher, remain unchanged, or fall in price. The idea is to keep the option premiums from the short calls, so a bullish move in the underlying instrument would result in losses.

5. A ratio put spread involves ______________.

   Answer: A—Buying a higher strike put option and selling a greater number of OTM put options.

   Discussion: The ratio put spread is similar to the ratio call spread. However, as the name suggests, the strategy uses puts instead of calls. In addition, the strategist is buying one or more put options and selling a greater number of puts with a lower strike price.

6. Calculate the values for the following ratio put spread:

   Long 1 January QQQ 35 Put @ 2.00

   Short 2 January QQQ 32 Puts @ 1.25

   Answer:

   Net credit = [(2 × 1.25) – 2] × 100 = $50 [(Short – long premium) × 100].

   Maximum profit = [(35 – 32) + .50] × 100 = $350 [(Difference in strike prices + net credit) × 100].

   Maximum risk = Limited to the downside until the underlying falls to zero ($2,850 is then the maximum loss).

   Downside breakeven = 35 – [(35 – 32) × 2) ÷ (2 – 1)] – .50 = $28.50 {Higher strike – [(difference in strike prices × number of short contracts) ÷ (number of short contracts – number of long contracts)] – net credit}.

   Discussion: The credit from the ratio put spread is equal to the premium received minus the premium paid, which, in this case, equals $2.50 minus $2.00, or $.50 per spread. The maximum profit occurs if the short options expire worthless but the long put increases in value as much as possible. At $32 a share at expiration, the short puts will expire worthless, but the long put will be worth $300. Therefore, the trader keeps all of the premium from the short puts, or $2.50, and makes another $1 profit on the long put. At that point, the maximum profit is $350. However, the risks are considerable and the maximum loss of $2,850 will occur if the underlying instrument falls to zero.

7. A ratio put spread should be implemented in a/an ______________ market.

   Answer: A—Bullish.

   Discussion: If the underlying asset makes a sharp drop, the ratio put spread will result in losses. For that reason, it is best established when the trader is bullish on the underlying instrument and expects to see a significant move higher or only a modest move lower.

8. True or False: Never attempt to place a ratio backspread in a market with low volatility.

   Answer: False.

   Discussion: Placing ratio backspreads in markets with low volatility is not recommended. However, if you do choose to trade a slow market, follow these three rules: (1) Use a .75 ratio or higher, (2) buy the lower strike, and (3) sell the higher strike.

9. A call ratio backspread involves ____________.

   Answer: B—Selling a lower strike call and buying a greater number of higher strike calls.

   Discussion: The call ratio backspread is established using call options. The strategist will simultaneously sell one or more calls and buy a greater number of calls with the same expiration date. Ratios of 1-to-2 or 2-to-3 are commonly used.

10. Calculate the values for the following call ratio backspread:

    Short 2 January QQQ 35 Calls @ 4.00

    Long 3 January QQQ 38 Calls @ 2.25

    Answer:

    Net credit = $[(2 \times 4) - (3 \times 2.25)] \times 100$ = \$125 [(Short – long premium) × 100].

    Maximum profit = Unlimited above the upside breakeven.

    Maximum risk = $[2 \times (38 - 35) - 1.25] \times 100$ = \$475 {[(Number of short calls × difference in strikes) – net credit] × 100}.

    Upside breakeven = $38 + [(38 - 35) \times 2] \div (3 - 2) - 1.25$ = \$42.75 {Higher strike + [(difference in strikes × number of short calls) ÷ (number of long calls – number of short calls)] – net credit}.

    Downside breakeven = $35 + 1.25$ = \$36.25 (Short strike + net credit).

    Discussion: The credit received, or debit paid, in a call ratio backspread equals the premium of the short options minus the premium for the long options—in this case, \$8.00 minus \$6.75, or \$125 per spread. The maximum profit is unlimited as the stock moves higher. A call ratio backspread is best placed in a market where you anticipate a sharp rise with increasing volatility.

11. Call ratio backspreads are best implemented during periods of ____________.

    Answer: C—Low volatility in a highly volatile market that shows signs of increasing activity to the upside.

Discussion: The call ratio backspread yields the greatest profits when the underlying instrument makes a significant move higher. If, however, the underlying instrument falls sharply, the strategist can keep the initial net credit. For that reason, it is best established for a credit, and this can usually be accomplished when volatility is low.

12. Put ratio backspreads are best implemented during periods of ________________.

    Answer: D—Low volatility in a highly volatile market that shows signs of increasing activity to the downside.

    Discussion: The put ratio backspread is a bearish strategy that generates the most profits when the underlying security makes an explosive move to the downside.

13. A put ratio backspread involves ______________.

    Answer: A—Selling a higher strike put and buying a greater number of lower strike puts.

    Discussion: The ratio put backspread is established by purchasing one or more puts and selling a greater number of puts with a lower strike price with the same expiration date. Ratios of 1-to-2 or 2-to-3 are often used to establish backspreads.

14. Calculate the values for the following put ratio backspread:

    Short 2 January QQQ 35 Puts @ 2.50

    Long 3 January QQQ 32 Puts @ 1.25

    Answer:

    Net credit = $[(2 \times 2.50) - (3 \times 1.25)] \times 100$ = \$125 [(Short – long premium) × 100].

    Maximum profit = \$2,725 (Limited to the downside as the underlying falls to zero).

    Maximum risk = $[2 \times (35 - 32)] - 1.25 \times 100$ = \$475 [(Number of short puts × difference in strikes) – net credit] × 100.

    Upside breakeven = $(35 - 1.25)$ = \$33.75 (Higher strike – net credit).

    Downside breakeven = $32 - [2 \times (35 - 32) \div (3 - 2)] + 1.25$ = \$27.25 {Lower strike – [(number of short puts × difference in strikes) ÷ (number of long puts – number of short puts)] + net credit}.

    Discussion: The net credit (or net debit) from the put ratio backspread is equal to the premium received minus the premium paid. If the underlying instrument rallies, the strategist can let the puts expire worthless and keep the net credit. The maximum profit, however, occurs if the underlying asset falls sharply. In this case, the maximum profit is equal to $2,725. The maximum risk, meanwhile, is limited and equal to the difference in the strike prices times the number of short options minus the net credit.

15. What is the difference between a forward and a reverse volatility skew?

    Answer: With a forward price skew, the options with the higher strike prices have higher implied volatility than the options with lower strike prices. The reverse volatility skew, in contrast, will have higher implied volatility in the lower strike prices when compared to the higher strike prices.

    Discussion: Ratio backspreads and other types of vertical spreads can take advantage of volatility skews. For example, with a forward skew, strategists can sell the options with the higher strike price and buy those with the lower strike price. On the other hand, strategists can buy the higher strike price and sell the lower one if a reverse volatility skew exists. The type of spread, and whether to use puts or calls, will depend on the outlook for the underlying asset. For instance, if a contract has a reverse skew and the strategist is bullish on the underlying asset, a call ratio backspread might be the appropriate strategy to employ.

MEDIA ASSIGNMENT

In this chapter, we once again use the free options calculator at the Chicago Board Options Exchange web site to create a risk curve (in Chapter 4 we created a curve for the long call). This chapter's example focuses on the call ratio backspread. Before plotting the graph, the reader should have generated a table similar to the one shown.

Stock Price	Long Call Price	Value of Two Long Calls	Value of Short Call	Position Value
60	0.45	0.90	2.20	−1.30
65	1.25	2.50	4.50	−2.00
70	2.80	5.60	7.80	−2.20
75	5.15	10.30	11.80	−1.50
80	8.40	16.80	16.25	0.55
85	12.30	24.60	21.00	3.60
90	16.50	33.00	26.00	7.00

After creating the table, plotting the risk curve is relatively straightforward. We plot the coordinates where the stock price (first column) and the value of the options trade (last column) intersect. For instance, when the stock price equals $85, the value of the call ratio backspread equals $3.60. Once all eight coordinates are plotted on the risk curve, connect the dots and the risk curve should look like the one shown in the figure.

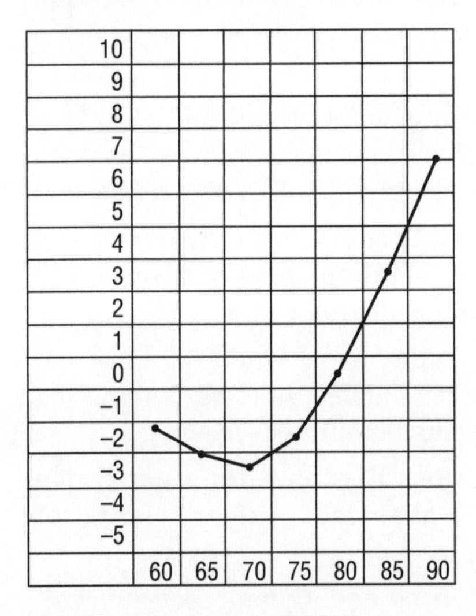

Call Ratio Backspread Risk Curve

VOCABULARY DEFINITIONS

Call ratio backpread: A spread that involves selling a call and buying a greater number of calls with a higher strike price and the same expiration month.

Forward volatility skew: A type of volatility skew in which the option with the higher strike price has a higher implied volatility than the option with the lower strike price.

Nondirectional: A type of options strategy that will profit whether the underlying asset moves higher or lower. Its success does not depend on a move in a specific direction. Straddles and strangles are examples of nondirectional trades.

Price skew: A type of volatility skew where options with the same expiration date, but different strike prices, have different levels of implied volatility.

Put ratio backspread: A strategy that involves selling a put option and buying a greater number of put options with a lower strike price. The expiration dates of all the put options are the same.

Ratio backspread: A spread in which more options are purchased than sold and where all options have the same underlying and expiration date, but different strike prices.

Ratio call spread: A spread strategy that involves buying a call and selling a greater number of calls with a lower strike price and the same expiration date.

Ratio put spread: A strategy of buying put options and selling a greater number of put options with the same expiration date but a lower strike price.

Ratio spread: A strategy that involves buying and selling options (all puts or all calls) with the same expiration date, but different strike prices. The number of long contracts and short contracts are not equal.

Reverse volatility skew: A type of volatility skew where options that have the same expiration date have higher implied volatility among the lower strike prices when compared to the higher strike prices.

Time skew: A type of skew where options that have the same strike prices, but different expiration dates, have vastly different levels of implied volatility.

Volatility skew: When options on the same underlying asset but with different strike prices and/or expiration dates have different levels of implied volatility. One of the most common volatility skews occurs when the short-term options have a much higher level of implied volatility compared to the longer-term options.

CHAPTER 10

Trading Techniques for Range-Bound Markets

SUMMARY

Sometimes the markets just don't move much. For many traders, the lack of direction or volatility can prove frustrating. After all, if markets are moving sideways, how can a trader generate profits from bullish or bearish strategies? Straddles and strangles won't work very well, either, as they require significant movement to cover the costs of the double option premium. Fortunately, there are a few options strategies that can generate profits in sideways-moving markets.

This chapter explores some of the strategies that can deliver profits when the underlying instrument trades quietly and without much movement. These approaches take advantage of the fact that options are wasting assets and lose value with the passage of time. Examples include the long butterfly, long condor, and the long iron butterfly, as well as calendar spreads and collars. These strategies can be used to profit from time decay and thus can help options traders generate profits even in low-volatility or range-bound markets.

Although the real excitement in trading may come from jumping on a big trend and watching your chosen stock double every month or your options double or triple by the end of the week, in the real world that seldom happens. If you accept the fact that the majority of stocks are not going to move significantly from month-to-month, you can make consistent, although modest, profits using sideways strategies. And since the risk is defined, you will not take on any more risk than is acceptable to you.

QUESTIONS AND EXERCISES

1. In sideways markets, option strategies can be developed to take advantage of ______________.
   A. Gamma decay.
   B. Theta decay.
   C. Delta neutrality.
   D. Vega neutrality.

2. A sideways market is a market that ______________.
   A. Has extremely low volatility.
   B. Moves erratically.
   C. Stays between consistent resistance and support levels.
   D. Stays at the same market volume consistently.

3. Name the three parts of a butterfly strategy.
   1. ______________________________
   2. ______________________________
   3. ______________________________

4. The body of a butterfly spread contains ______________.
   A. An option with the strike price above the resistance level.
   B. An option with the strike price below the support level.
   C. An option with the strike price outside of the support and resistance levels.
   D. An option with the strike price in between the support and resistance levels.

5. The wings of a butterfly spread are comprised of ______________.
   A. Options with the strike prices outside of the trading range.
   B. Options with the strike prices at both ends of the trading range.
   C. Options with the strike prices close to the equilibrium level.
   D. One option outside the support level and one inside the resistance level.

6. A long butterfly spread consists of ______________.
   A. Going long (buying) the wings and going short (selling) the body (the middle strike options).
   B. Going long (buying) the wings and going long (buying) the body (the middle strike options).
   C. Going short (selling) the wings and going long (buying) the body (the middle strike options).
   D. Going short (selling) the wings and going short (selling) the body (the middle strike options).

7. Money is made on a long butterfly when the market closes ______________.
   A. Outside of the wings.
   B. In-between the wings.

8. Calculate the values for the following long butterfly trade:

   Long 1 December IBM 80 Call @ 7.50

   Short 2 December IBM 85 Calls @ 5.00

   Long 1 December IBM 90 Call @ 3.00

   IBM is currently trading at $85.

   Net debit = ______________________________

   Maximum reward = ______________________________

   Maximum risk = ______________________________

   Upside breakeven = ______________________________

   Downside breakeven = ______________________________

9. In a long condor, you need to ______________.
   A. Go long the two inner option strikes of the body and go long the wings.
   B. Go long the two inner option strikes of the body and go short the wings.
   C. Go short the two inner option strikes of the body and go long the wings.
   D. Go short the two inner option strikes of the body and go short the wings.

10. Calculate the values for the following long condor trade:

    Long 1 MSFT December 60 Call @ 8.00

    Short 1 MSFT December 65 Call @ 5.00

    Short 1 MSFT December 70 Call @ 2.00

    Long 1 MSFT December 75 Call @ 1.00

    Net debit = ______________________________

    Maximum reward = ______________________________

    Maximum risk = ______________________________

    Upside breakeven = ______________________________

    Downside breakeven = ______________________________

11. A long iron butterfly is a combination of ____________________.

    A. A bear put spread and a bull put spread.

    B. A bear call spread and a bull call spread.

    C. A bear call spread and a bull put spread.

    D. A bear put spread and a bull call spread.

12. Calculate the values for the following long iron butterfly trade:

    Long 1 EBAY January 75 Call @ $2.50

    Short 1 EBAY January 70 Call @ $5.00

    Short 1 EBAY January 65 Put @ $2.00

    Long 1 EBAY January 60 Put @ $1.00

    Net credit = ______________________________

    Maximum reward = ______________________________

    Maximum risk = ______________________________

    Upside breakeven = ______________________________

    Downside breakeven = ______________________________

13. A calendar spread is a combination of ____________________.

    A. A long option and a short option.

    B. A covered call and a protective put.

14. A diagonal spread is a combination of ____________.
    A. A long option and a short option.
    B. A covered call and a protective put.

15. A collar strategy is a combination of ____________.
    A. A long option and a short option.
    B. A covered call and a protective put.

MEDIA ASSIGNMENT

In this chapter, we are going to look for stocks that are trading sideways or within a range. In order to do so, connect to the Internet with your browser set on www.optionetics.com. At that point, you'll see the "Free Ranker" on the Optionetics home page. At the time of this writing, it is located near the bottom right-hand side of the web site.

Using the free ranker, you want to look for range-bound stocks. In this effort, you can click on the button that says "Quiet." These stocks are the ones that have less volatility relative to historical levels. To be specific, the quiet ranking sorts stocks based on the six-day statistical volatility compared to the 100-day. According to the site, "These stocks are candidates for sideways trades like calendar spreads and butterflies."

VOCABULARY LIST

Body
Butterfly
Calendar spread
Collar
Condor
Diagonal spread
Directionless
Equilibrium level
Iron butterfly
Range-bound
Resistance
Sideways
Support
Theta
Time decay
Trading range
Wasting asset
Wings

SOLUTIONS

1. In sideways markets, option strategies can be developed to take advantage of ____________.

   Answer: B—Theta decay.

   Discussion: Theta is a Greek letter used to define how an options price will change due to the passage of time. It is another term for time decay, which refers to the fact that option premiums lose value as the expiration date draws closer.

2. A sideways market is a market that ____________.

   Answer: C—Stays between consistent resistance and support levels.

   Discussion: A sideways or range-bound market is the opposite of a trending market. It is a period of quiet trading that sees little price movement in the underlying asset. Traders often use technical support and resistance levels to identify the trading range of a sideways market.

3. Name the three parts of a butterfly strategy.

   Answer: Upper wing, body, and lower wing.

   Discussion: With a long butterfly, the strategist sells two at-the-money options and buys an in-the-money and an out-of-the money option. In that case, the at-the-money options are considered the body. The option with the higher strike price is the upper wing and the option with the lower strike price is the lower wing.

4. The body of a butterfly spread contains ____________.

   Answer: D—An option with the strike price in between the support and resistance levels.

   Discussion: Ideally, the strategist will use technical support and resistance levels to identify the best strike prices to use for the body of the butterfly spread.

5. The wings of a butterfly spread are comprised of ____________.

   Answer: B—Options with the strike prices at both ends of the trading range.

   Discussion: Establishing the wings using strike prices near the upper and lower ends of the trading range will help increase the odds of success when establishing long butterflies. Ideally, if the underlying instrument revisits the upper or lower bands of the trading range, it will revert and head back toward the strike price of the body.

6. A long butterfly spread consists of ______________.

   Answer: A—Going long (buying) the wings and going short (selling) the body (the middle strike options).

   Discussion: With a long butterfly, the strategist sells two at-the-money options and buys an in-the-money and an out-of-the money option.

7. Money is made on a long butterfly when the market closes ______________.

   Answer: B—In-between the wings.

   Discussion: Ideally, the underlying instrument will stay within a trading range. If it moves towards the middle strike prices (of the short options), the short options will expire worthless and the strategist can keep the premium.

8. Calculate the values for the following long butterfly trade:

   Long 1 December IBM 80 Call @ 7.50

   Short 2 December IBM 85 Calls @ 5.00

   Long 1 December IBM 90 Call @ 3.00

   IBM is currently trading at $85.

   Answer:

   Net debit = [(7.50 + 3) – (2 × 5)] × 100 = $50 [(Long – short premiums) × 100].

   Maximum reward = [(85 – 80) – .50] × 100 = $450 [(Difference between strikes – net debit) × 100].

   Maximum risk = $50 (Limited to the net debit paid).

   Upside breakeven = (90 – .50) = $89.50 (Highest strike – net debit).

   Downside breakeven = (80 + .50) = $80.50 (Lowest strike + net debit).

   Discussion: The long butterfly is a limited risk strategy with a maximum loss equal to the net debit paid. The maximum reward is equal to the difference between highest strike and the short strike minus the net debit. Maximum profit is realized when the stock price equals the short strike. The upside breakeven equals the highest strike price minus the net debit paid, and the downside breakeven equals the lowest strike price plus the net debit paid.

9. In a long condor, you need to _____________.

Answer: C—Go short the two inner option strikes of the body and go long the wings.

Discussion: Just as with the long butterfly, the long condor involves selling two options and buying two options. However, the options that are sold will have two different strike prices; so with the long condor, the strategist is buying four separate contracts.

10. Calculate the values for the following long condor trade:

Long 1 MSFT December 60 Call @ 8.00

Short 1 MSFT December 65 Call @ 5.00

Short 1 MSFT December 70 Call @ 2.00

Long 1 MSFT December 75 Call @ 1.00

Answer:

Net debit = [(8 + 1) – (5 + 2)] × 100 = $200 [(Long – short premiums) × 100].

Maximum reward = [(35 – 30) – 2] × 100 = $300 [(Difference between strikes – net debit) × 100].

Maximum risk = $200 (Limited to the net debit).

Upside breakeven (75 – 2) = $73 (Highest strike – net debit).

Downside breakeven (60 + 2) = $62 (Lowest strike + net debit).

Discussion: The maximum risk of the long condor is the debit paid. The best reward is equal to the difference between the strike prices minus the net debit. The upside breakeven is equal to the highest strike price minus the net debit. The lowest strike price is equal to the downside breakeven plus the net debit.

11. A long iron butterfly is a combination of _____________.

Answer: C—A bear call spread and a bull put spread.

Discussion: The long iron butterfly is a strategy that consists of four options with the same expiration date and different strike prices. To establish the trade, the strategist will buy one higher strike call and sell one lower strike call, which is the same as a bear call spread. The strategist will also sell a put and buy a lower strike put, which is the same as a bull put spread. The short puts and calls will be at- or near-the-money. The long puts and calls will be out-of-the-money. The idea is to see the underlying asset stay in a range and for the short options to expire with little or no value. The long options serve as a hedge in the event of a significant move higher or lower in the underlying asset.

12. Calculate the values for the following long iron butterfly trade:

    Long 1 EBAY January 75 Call @ $2.50

    Short 1 EBAY January 70 Call @ $5.00

    Short 1 EBAY January 65 Put @ $2.00

    Long 1 EBAY January 60 Put @ $1.00

    Answer:

    Net credit = [(5 + 2) – (2.50 + 1)] × 100 = $350 [(Short – long premiums) × 100].

    Maximum reward = $350 (Limited to the net credit).

    Maximum risk = [(75 – 70) – 3.50] × 100 = $150 [(Difference between long and short strikes – net credit) × 100].

    Upside breakeven = (70 + 3.50) = $73.50 (Strike price of upper short call + net credit).

    Downside breakeven = (65 – 3.50) = $61.50 (Strike price of lower short put—net credit).

    Discussion: The long iron butterfly is established for a credit, which is equal to the premium received for the short options minus the premium paid for the long options. The maximum reward is the net credit. The maximum risk is equal to the difference between the strike prices minus the credit. The upside breakeven equals the short call strike price plus the credit. The downside breakeven equals the strike price of the short put minus the credit.

13. A calendar spread is a combination of ______________.

    Answer: A—A long option and a short option.

    Discussion: In the calendar spread, the strategist is buying a long-term option and also selling a short-term option. Both options have the same strike prices, but different expiration dates. Calendar spreads can be created with either puts or calls.

14. A diagonal spread is a combination of ______________.

    Answer: A—A long option and a short option.

    Discussion: Diagonal spreads can be constructed in different ways. In any situation, however, the strategist is buying an option and also selling an option. The options will have different expiration dates and different strike prices. For instance, a diagonal spread can be created by purchasing a longer-term out-of-the-money call and simultaneously selling a shorter-term at-the-money call.

15. A collar strategy is a combination of ___________.

Answer: B—A covered call and a protective put.

Discussion: A collar is created around a stock by purchasing a put option and selling a call option. In most cases, both the call and the put will be out-of-the-money. The strategy is similar to the protective put, but the cost of the put is offset with the sale of a call. The collar has limited risks and limited rewards.

MEDIA ASSIGNMENT

This chapter encourages readers to visit the Optionetics.com home page and use the free ranker to search for stocks with low volatility. By clicking on the "Quiet" button, readers can generate a list of stocks that have relatively low levels of statistical volatility relative to the past. Subscribers using Optionetics.com Platinum will be able to provide more refined screens that can produce a list of low-volatility stocks. Often, these companies are in industries with stable profits like consumer products, groceries, or pharmaceuticals.

It is often helpful to generate a price chart of promising stocks. By charting the quiet stocks, traders should be able to identify support and resistance levels, which can also help identify potential candidates for the various range-bound strategies discussed in this chapter. As usual, new traders are encouraged to paper trade and back-test these strategies for range-bound markets before actually putting money on the line.

VOCABULARY DEFINITIONS

Body: The inner part of a butterfly spread. In the case of the long butterfly, it represents the options that are being sold and that have strike prices between the highest and lowest strike prices.

Butterfly: The sale (or purchase) of two identical options, together with the purchase (or sale) of one option with an immediately higher strike and one option with an immediately lower strike. All options must be the same type, have the same underlying, and have the same expiration date.

Calendar spread: A spread consisting of the purchase of one long-term option and the sale of one short-term option of the same type with the same exercise price.

Collar: A type of strategy that involves buying shares, selling calls, and buying puts. It is a combination of a covered call and a protective put.

Condor: The sale (or purchase) of two options with consecutive exercise prices, together with the purchase (or sale) of one option with an immediately lower exercise price and one option with an immediately higher exercise price.

Diagonal spread: A two-sided spread consisting of buying a long-term option and selling a shorter-term option with different strike prices. Options are of the same type and have the same underlying asset.

Directionless: Refers to an investment that lacks direction and is not trending higher or lower. Certain options strategies work well when the underlying asset is not moving higher or lower (i.e., when it is directionless).

Equilibrium level: The level where supply meets demand. The mean between an asset's support price and resistance price.

Iron butterfly: The combination of a long (or short) straddle and a short (or long) strangle. All options must have the same underlying and have the same expiration.

Range-bound: Refers to an investment or market that is not trending higher or lower, but rather remaining within a narrow price span.

Resistance: A price level that serves as a ceiling to higher prices. A stock might turn away from this price level on a few occasions.

Sideways: An investment or market that lacks clear direction and tends to show relatively little price change.

Support: A price level at which a stock or market begins seeing increasing demand or buying interest. It serves as a floor to lower prices. A major support area is one that has been tested on several occasions and over a sustained period of time. When a major support area is broken and the stock or market begins to falter, a more meaningful move to the downside may occur. For that reason, technicians consider major support areas to be significant.

Theta: The Greek letter that refers to the loss in an option's value due to the passage of time. Theta is expressed as a number such as –.10 or –.05.

Time decay: The process of options losing value as the expiration date approaches.

Trading range: The recent high and low prices of a stock or other investment that serve as resistance and support.

Wasting asset: An investment that loses value over time. Options have set expiration dates and lose value as time passes, so they are considered wasting assets.

Wings: A term to describe a portion of a butterfly or condor. In a long butterfly, for instance, the wings are the options that are purchased and have the highest and lowest strike prices. The body consists of the short options with the middle strike prices.

CHAPTER 11

Increasing Your Profits with Adjustments

SUMMARY

Experienced options traders are continuously assessing the risk/reward profile of open positions because as the underlying asset changes in value, so will other factors. For instance, the delta of a position can change dramatically as the underlying asset moves higher or lower. So, to stay delta neutral in a strategy like a long synthetic straddle, an options strategist must often make modifications to the position. This may include buying more contracts or shares or selling them. When a strategist makes changes to a position due to price movements in the underlying asset, the strategist is making an adjustment to the position. The strategist does not need to tell the broker that an adjustment is being made. Instead, the trader simply enters the order to buy or sell more options or shares in order to bring the position back to delta neutral.

This chapter explores the process of adjustments. For instance, how do changes in the market influence the overall position delta of the trade? If the move is significant, it might be time to adjust the trade. Often, by making an adjustment, a trader can increase profits on the trade by bringing the trade back to delta neutral. In addition, adjustments can be made to lock in profits or to help salvage the value of a losing trade. The most important factor to understand is that option positions are not just opened and closed. In many cases, they can be modified with adjustments to improve their overall risk/reward profiles.

QUESTIONS AND EXERCISES

1. Name three things you can do when the market moves and your trade is no longer delta neutral.

   1. ______________________________
   2. ______________________________
   3. ______________________________

2. An adjustment can be made by ______________ to offset your position to bring it back to delta neutral.

   A. Buying or selling options.
   B. Buying or selling futures.
   C. Buying or selling stocks.
   D. All of the above.

3. Name the two sides of a delta neutral trade.

   1. ______________________________
   2. ______________________________

4. Stock has a ______________ delta.

   A. Fixed.
   B. Variable.
   C. Fixed or variable.

5. Options have ______________ deltas.

   A. Fixed.
   B. Variable.
   C. Fixed or variable.

6. ATM options are easy to work with because they have ______________.

   A. Low liquidity and thin price spreads.
   B. Low liquidity and large price spreads.
   C. High liquidity and thin price spreads.
   D. High liquidity and large price spreads.

7. Time-based adjustments are based on ______________.

   A. The number of days left until expiration.
   B. Regular intervals (days, weeks, months, etc.).

   C. The movements of the sun.
   D. All of the above.

8. Event-based adjustments are most likely to occur _____________.
   A. When a special event dictates the adjustment.
   B. At regular intervals (days, weeks, months, etc.).
   C. Based on an expected event that is known beforehand.
   D. All of the above.

9. What is the key advantage of using an at-the-money option?
   A. It will have several strike prices.
   B. It is more likely to have high open interest and liquidity.
   C. The strike price will be slightly above the market value of the underlying instrument.
   D. The strike price will be slightly below the market value of the underlying instrument.

10. Calls have _____________ deltas.
    A. Negative.
    B. Fixed.
    C. Positive.
    D. None of the above.

11. Puts have _____________ deltas.
    A. Negative.
    B. Fixed.
    C. Positive.
    D. None of the above.

MEDIA ASSIGNMENT

In this media assignment, we are going to return to the free options calculator at the Chicago Board Options Exchange (CBOE) and compute the deltas of various options positions. Once your PC is booted and online, type www.cboe.com into the web browser, which will take you to the Chicago Board Options Exchange web site. From the CBOE home page, click the "Trading Tools" tab, then the "Volatility Optimizer," and then click on "Options Calculator." Next, select "American" in the style box. (*Note:* If the calculator on the CBOE site is not available, readers can use any options calculator that includes the variable delta to complete this assignment.)

Next, input some variables into the calculator. First, let the stock price equal 60 and the strike price equal 75; the volatility is 30 percent, the annual interest rate is 5 percent, and the company pays no dividend (quarterly dividend amount equals 0). Next, in the "Days Left to Expiration" box, click "Days Until Expiration" and enter the number 100. We are going to look at an options contract with 100 days remaining until expiration that has a strike price of 75 and volatility of 30 percent, with an underlying security trading at $60 that pays no dividends. Now, write down the delta of the put and the delta of the call.

Let's assume that the stock price begins to climb higher. Change the equity price to 70. What are the deltas now? What about at 75? Now, assume we buy a straddle using one put and one call. What is the delta of this position? Or, assume that we buy 100 shares and buy two puts. What is the position delta? Finally, assume that the stock price climbs to 80. What are the deltas of the put and the call? What are the position deltas of the straddle and the long synthetic straddle? In the case of the straddle, what can we do to get back to delta neutral?

VOCABULARY LIST

Adjustment

Directional trade

Event-based adjustment

Fixed delta

Liquidity

Negative delta

Open interest

Positive delta

Thin spreads

Time-based adjustment

Variable delta

SOLUTIONS

1. Name three things you can do when the market moves and your trade is no longer delta neutral.

   Answer: Exit the trade, maintain the trade as is, or make an adjustment.

   Discussion: There are advantages and disadvantages to each of the three courses of action. So, ultimately, the best alternative will depend on the specific situation. Since the key to profitable trading lies in assessing the available choices, learning the benefits of adjusting can help you to become a more profitable trader.

2. An adjustment can be made by ______________ to offset your position to bring it back to delta neutral.

   Answer: D—All of the above (buying or selling options, futures, or stocks).

   Discussion: Delta neutral trades are created by simultaneously purchasing (or selling) the underlying asset (stocks, futures, exchange-traded funds, etc.) along with the purchase (or sale) of options contracts.

3. Name the two sides of a delta neutral trade.

   Answer: Hedge and directional bet.

   Discussion: You can think of a delta neutral position as two trades. The first is a directional bet on a market, stock, or futures contract. The other is a hedge in case the directional bet goes awry.

4. Stock has a ______________ delta.

   Answer: A—Fixed.

   Discussion: Delta is the measure of the price change of a derivative relative to the price change of an underlying asset. The delta of an options contract can change as the price of the underlying asset moves higher or lower. It varies. However, stocks (and futures contracts) always have a delta equal to 100. If a stock price moves up $1, the position increases in value by $1 times the number of shares. It never varies; it is fixed.

5. Options have ______________ deltas.

   Answer: B—Variable.

   Discussion: Each options contract has a unique delta that changes over time. It can range between 0 and 100. An option with a high delta will move very much like the price of the underlying asset. For instance, a contract with a delta of 100 will experience a one-to-one price movement with the price changes of the underlying asset. Importantly, however, the delta can change over time. It is variable.

6. ATM options are easy to work with because they have ______________.

   Answer: C—High liquidity and thin price spreads.

   Discussion: At-the-money options tend to attract the most amount of interest and are often more liquid than other strike prices for that reason. The spreads, or difference between bids and offers, will often be smaller as well. This is especially true for the near-term or front-month options.

7. Time-based adjustments are based on ______________.

   Answer: B—Regular intervals (days, weeks, months, etc.).

   Discussion: Strategists sometimes use regular time intervals to decide when to adjust a position. For instance, a trader might decide to adjust the position every two weeks. This is an example of a time-based adjustment.

8. Event-based adjustments are most likely to occur ______________.

   Answer: A—When a special event dictates the adjustment.

   Discussion: Some options traders wait for a specific event to dictate when an adjustment should be implemented on an open position. Earnings announcements, takeover talk, and management shake-ups are examples of events that might trigger an adjustment to an open stock option position.

9. What is the key advantage of using an at-the-money option?

   Answer: B—It is more likely to have high open interest and liquidity.

   Discussion: At-the-money options tend to have higher levels of open interest when compared to other strike prices. High open interest, in turn, is a sign of liquidity and robust levels of trading activity. These options tend to be more liquid than others.

10. Calls have ____________ deltas.

    Answer: C—Positive.

    Discussion: As the price of the underlying asset moves higher, the call will appreciate in value. Thus, the call option has a positive delta. Calls move in the same direction as the price of the underlying asset.

11. Puts have ____________ deltas.

    Answer: A—Negative.

    Discussion: As the price of the underlying asset moves higher, the put option will lose value. As the price of the underlying asset falls, the put will increase in value. Therefore, puts have negative deltas. They move in the opposite direction to the price of the underlying asset.

MEDIA ASSIGNMENT

In this chapter, readers are encouraged to use the options calculator at the Chicago Board Options Exchange to find the deltas of a call, a put, a straddle, and a long synthetic straddle. Readers should notice that as the stock price moves higher, the delta of the call increases. Meanwhile, the delta of the put also increases (becomes less negative). Using the numbers provided would produce a table similar to the one shown.

Stock Price	Call Delta	Put Delta
60	0.10	−0.97
70	0.39	−0.63
75	0.57	−0.45
80	0.72	−0.29

The reader is also asked to compute the delta of the straddle when the stock price equals the strike price of 75. At that time, the position would have a delta of +12 (57 – 45). The long synthetic straddle, which would include 100 shares and two puts, would have a positive delta of 100 minus 45 minus 45, or +10. Finally, the last question asks to compute the position deltas of the straddle and the long synthetic straddle when the stock price reaches 80. In that case, the straddle would have a delta of 43 (72 – 29) and the long synthetic straddle would have a delta of 42 (100 – 29 – 29). So, what could the strategist do with the long synthetic straddle to move the position closer to delta neutral? Buy one more put, which would give the position a delta of only +13.

VOCABULARY DEFINITIONS

Adjustment: Making a change to a trade in order to bring it back to delta neutral and alter the reward/risk ratio. Traders often make adjustments to delta neutral strategies like long straddles and long synthetic straddles.

Directional trade: A trade that requires the underlying asset to move in one direction in order to produce profits. To make a profit, the trader must determine before placing a directional trade which way the asset will go. Buying stocks is an example of a directional bet because the stock price must move higher in order to generate profits.

Event-based adjustment: A type of adjustment to an options contract that is based on a specific event like an earnings announcement, a profit report, or a management change.

Fixed delta: A delta figure that does not change due to any price changes. Stocks and futures contracts have a fixed delta of plus or minus 100.

Liquidity: The ease with which an asset can be converted to cash in the marketplace. A large number of buyers and sellers and a high volume of trading activity provide high liquidity. Liquidity is a concern for any moneys that may be required on short notice, whether for emergencies or for planned purchases.

Negative delta: A delta that moves opposite to the price of the underlying asset. For instance, a put has a negative delta because as the underlying asset moves higher, the value of the put moves lower.

Open interest: The total number of options contracts that have been opened and not yet closed out.

Positive delta: A delta that moves in the same direction as the underlying asset. Calls, for example, have positive deltas because they appreciate as the underlying asset moves higher.

Thin spreads: Large gaps between the bids and offers caused by infrequent and illiquid trading. Thin spreads tend to move a great deal and will often move against the trader once an order is submitted.

Time-based adjustment: A type of modification to an options contract that occurs at regular intervals (five days, two weeks, one month, etc.). Strategists sometimes use time-based adjustments to keep positions delta neutral.

Variable delta: A delta that changes as the price of the underlying asset moves higher or lower. Options have variable deltas.

CHAPTER 12

Choosing the Right Broker

SUMMARY

Choosing the right broker can be a difficult task, but it can also prove to be one of the most important trading decisions that you can make. New traders will often choose a broker based on the fees charged (i.e., the cheaper, the better). Yet, while keeping trading costs low is an important factor to consider, other aspects of the broker's responsibilities and accessible tools—such as the quality of executions, online tools, and research—can prove equally important over the long run.

In this chapter, we hope to help you determine what defines the right broker for you. First, it's important to understand how brokers operate, their roles and responsibilities, and what separates the quality brokers from the inferior firms. In addition, there are several different types of brokers. Some offer rock-bottom commissions, but nothing else. Others specialize in a specific investment (stocks, bonds, mutual funds, etc.), and some offer one-stop shopping to solve a variety of financial needs. Choosing from the wide array of brokers available today often requires a look at your needs as a trader in order to determine which one is right for you.

QUESTIONS AND EXERCISES

1. Define the word *broker*.

____

____

2. What is the primary difference between a self-directed broker and a full-service broker?

____

____

3. When you buy or sell a security through a brokerage firm, you pay ____________.
   A. A commission.
   B. Interest.
   C. Nothing.
   D. None of the above.

4. What is an advantage of using an online broker?
   A. In most cases, you can place trades through a live broker if you need to.
   B. Commission costs are cheaper.
   C. Online brokers often provide a wide range of research, investment tools, and information.
   D. All of the above.

5. A *fill* is a Wall Street term meaning ____________.
   A. What traders do on their lunch break.
   B. The execution (price) of a trade.
   C. When too many orders are submitted at once.
   D. The price charged in addition to the commission.

6. Many options traders focus on commissions, but ____________ can be just as important.
   A. Interest charges.
   B. Quality of executions.
   C. Location.
   D. Freebies.

7. Payment for order flow ____________.
   A. Always leads to the best execution.
   B. Is often a conflict of interest for the brokerage firm.
   C. Can lead to poor fills.

D. A and B.

E. B and C.

8. The duty of best execution ______________.

A. Requires brokerage firms to work for their clients and shop for the best available prices.

B. Is the responsibility of the trader, not the broker.

C. Is a rule imposed by the Options Clearing Corporation.

D. All of the above.

9. If a broker encourages a client to do many trades in order to generate more commissions, the broker is ______________.

A. Churning the account.

B. Failing to live up to the duty of best execution.

C. Involved in payment for order flow.

D. None of the above.

10. Front running is ______________.

A. A violation of current regulations.

B. The practice of trading ahead of customer's orders.

C. The misuse of privileged information.

D. All of the above.

11. In order to open an options trading account with most brokerage firms, new customers must ______________.

A. Demonstrate a sufficient amount of investment experience.

B. Complete the options approval form.

C. Have a certain net worth.

D. All of the above.

12. SEC stands for the ______________.

MEDIA ASSIGNMENT

In order to learn more about brokers, let's get online and find some information. There is plenty of free information out there. One starting place is the brokerage review section at Optionetics.com. To access the site, visit www.optionetics.com and look for the tab that says "Broker Review." From there, you can compare brokers based on commission charges, online trading capabilities, and options usefulness. The brokerage review section provides profiles for a dozen or so leading brokerage firms: the firms' online trading capabilities, the commissions, any research tools available, and important tidbits such as telephone numbers, locations, and each firm's web site address.

After looking through the broker review section, visit the web sites of some brokerage firms that interest you. Most brokerage sites offer information about trading demos, charting capabilities, research tools, special offers, and other information specific to that brokerage firm. Once you open a brokerage account, you could be with that firm for many years, even decades. So, take some time in the beginning to find the one that is right for you.

Finally, keep an eye out for information about brokerage firms in various news sources. A number of financial publications and web sites also conduct annual rankings of brokerage firms. *Barron's* provides a regular review of various brokerage firms (see, for instance, the article "Trading Up," by Theresa Carey, March 8, 2004). In the spring of 2004, the weekly publication picked OptionsXpress as its top online broker. However, the rankings change from year-to-year. To stay current, look for the latest articles and do a web search using keywords like "best brokers" or "top brokerage firms."

VOCABULARY LIST

Broker

Broker-assisted trade

Broker/dealer

Churning

Clearinghouse

Commission

Discount broker

Duty of best execution

Execution

Fill

Front running

Full-service broker

Hedge fund

Inside information

Insider trading

Institutional investor

Listed/listing

Live broker

National Association of Securities Dealers (NASD)

Online broker

Options approval form

Options Clearing Corporation (OCC)

Order

Payment for order flow

Privileged information

Retail investor

Securities and Exchange Commission (SEC)

Self-directed broker

Series 7

Ticket

SOLUTIONS

1. Define the word *broker*.

   Answer: A broker is an individual or entity that is licensed to buy and sell marketplace securities and/or derivatives to traders and investors.

   Discussion: *Broker* is a term used rather loosely to describe either a firm or an individual that is authorized to trade investment securities. If your next-door neighbor tells you that he or she works as a broker, he or she probably has passed the Series 7 licensing exam, which gives him or her the authority to take orders for stocks, bonds, and mutual funds. However, brokers must also work with firms that are regulated by the Securities and Exchange Commission and the National Association of Securities Dealers.

2. What is the primary difference between a self-directed broker and a full-service broker?

   Answer: Full-service brokers offer advice in addition to executing orders. Self-directed brokerage firms are for investors or traders who make their own decisions.

   Discussion: A full-service firm can provide you with investment tools, information and advice that is not available at self-directed firms. However, these services come at a cost. In most cases, the cost is in the form of higher commissions. Therefore, do-it-yourself investors who are seeking lower commissions often use self-directed firms.

3. When you buy or sell a security through a brokerage firm, you pay ______________.

   Answer: A—A commission.

   Discussion: The primary source of revenue for many brokerage firms is the commissions from trading. Individual brokers often make a living from commissions. When a client buys an investment security, he or she is charged a commission. When the client sells that security, he or she is also charged a commission.

4. What is an advantage of using an online broker?

   Answer: D—All of the above (in most cases, you can place trades through a live broker if you need to; commission costs are cheaper; online brokers often provide a wide range of research, investment tools, and information).

   Discussion: Most online brokers allow you to trade online or through a live broker. Generally, there is a higher commission imposed for broker-assisted trades. Nevertheless, commissions at online firms are generally cheaper than with full-service brokers. In addition, in order to compete with one another, many online brokerage firms provide a wide range of research, investment tools, and information.

5. A *fill* is a Wall Street term meaning ______________.

   Answer: B—The execution (price) of a trade.

   Discussion: On Wall Street, the term *fill* refers to the execution of a trade. For instance, "That was a good fill on my order for IBM calls" or "I was filled on my IBM order at $50 a share."

6. Many options traders focus on commissions, but ______________ can be just as important.

   Answer: B—Quality of executions.

   Discussion: Poor executions can often cost a trader more money than higher commissions. Ideally, a trader looks for a broker who will offer both great executions and rock-bottom commissions. In the real world, however, there is often a trade-off between the two.

7. Payment for order flow ______________.

   Answer: E—B and C (is often a conflict of interest for the brokerage firm and can lead to poor fills).

   Discussion: Payment for order flow describes the practice of sending orders to specific exchanges and receiving a cash payment for these orders. Brokerage firms that engage in this practice often face a conflict of interest because, since they receive a payment for routing an order to a specific exchange, they might not be sending the order to the exchange that is showing the best prices. For that reason, clients sometimes don't get the best executions when brokerage firms receive payments for orders.

8. The duty of best execution ______________.

   Answer: A—Requires brokerage firms to work for their clients and shop for the best available prices.

   Discussion: Brokerage firms have a duty of best execution, which requires them to try to get the best prices on all customer orders. In the options market, where options are listed on multiple exchanges, this often involves sending the order to the exchange showing the best prices.

9. If a broker encourages a client to do many trades in order to generate more commissions, the broker is ______________.

   Answer: A—Churning the account.

   Discussion: When a broker encourages a client to make frequent and sometimes unwarranted transactions within the client's account, the broker may be guilty of churning the account. This practice is prohibited and, if found guilty, the broker could face disciplinary action.

10. Front running is ______________.

    Answer: D—All of the above (a violation of current regulations, the practice of trading ahead of customers' orders, the misuse of privileged information).

    Discussion: Front running, the practice of trading ahead of a customer's orders, is generally not an important issue with small orders. However, front running ahead of large orders can be significant. For instance, if a trader at a brokerage firm knows that a large institutional client is going to buy a million shares of XYZ, that trader might buy XYZ ahead of the order because the stock price will probably go up once the order is executed. However, this type of front running is a violation of current regulations and also represents the misuse of privileged information.

11. In order to open an options trading account with most brokerage firms, new customers must ______________.

    Answer: D—All of the above (demonstrate a sufficient amount of investment experience, complete the options approval form, and have a certain net worth).

    Discussion: In order to begin trading options, a new customer must open an account and submit an options approval form. Among other things, brokerage firms look at clients' experience level and net worth before allowing them to trade options or certain high-risk strategies.

12. SEC stands for the ____________.

 Answer: Securities and Exchange Commission.

 Discussion: The Securities and Exchange Commission was created by Congress to regulate the securities markets and protect investors. It consists of five commissioners appointed by the President of the United States and approved by the Senate. Most traders simply refer to the commission as the SEC.

MEDIA ASSIGNMENT

After completing the media assignment in this chapter, readers should have a large amount of information regarding online brokers. The Broker Review section at www.optionetics.com provides information on the top online brokerage firms. In addition, after visiting various web sites of the individual brokers, readers should look for the annual rankings of brokerage firms in *Barron's* as well as other financial publications. From there, readers should be able to identify the two or three firms that best meet their needs, open options trading accounts, and begin trading.

VOCABULARY DEFINITIONS

Broker: A person or firm that buys and sells securities for customers. Most brokers charge commissions for executing transactions for customers.

Broker-assisted trade: A trade that is handled by a live broker. Many online brokerage firms allow customers not only to trade over the Internet, but also to talk to a live broker for assistance.

Broker/dealer: Another term used for brokerage firms or brokers.

Churning: Excessive trading in a customer's account by a broker who seeks to increase commissions. The practice is a violation of NASD regulations.

Clearinghouse: An institution established separately from the stock exchanges that ensures that the payment and delivery of stocks or options is handled accurately and efficiently.

Commission: A charge for executing a trade. Most brokerage firms charge commissions on stock and options transactions.

Discount broker: A brokerage firm that offers lower commission rates than a full-service broker, but does not offer services such as advice, research, and portfolio planning.

Duty of best execution: Brokerage firms have the obligation to look for the best prices for their customers. This often involves executing trades promptly or sending the order to the exchange that is currently showing the best quotes.

Execution: The process of completing an order to buy or sell a security. Once a trade is executed, it is reported in a confirmation report.

Fill: The execution of an order; also, the price at which an order is executed.

Front running: Broker practice of placing an order ahead of a customer's order. This practice can represent a conflict of interest and is prohibited.

Full-service broker: A type of stockbroker who provides more than stock quotes and order execution, including (and not limited to) portfolio planning and management, investment ideas, and researching specific investments. Since these brokers provide more than order taking and stock quotes, their commissions are higher.

Hedge fund: A private investment partnership that can use leverage and derivatives, take both long and short positions, and invest in many markets. Hedge funds can succeed in any market environment, even one with sharply declining prices, because they can take advantage of many speculative strategies, including program trading, swaps, arbitrage, and selling short.

Inside information: Relevant information about a company that has not yet been made public. It is illegal for holders of this information to make trades based on it, however received.

Insider trading: Making investment decisions based on information that is not yet public. Although trading based on this type of inside information does occur, it is against regulations.

Institutional investor: A customer at a brokerage firm or an investor that makes investment decisions for a large financial institution or hedge fund. Examples include portfolio managers, some professional financial advisers, mutual fund managers, and hedge fund traders.

Listed/Listing: Refers to the exchange where an investment trades. An investment is "listed" if it is traded on an exchange. For instance, companies pay fees to be traded on an exchange and must abide by the rules and regulations set out by the exchange to maintain listing privileges.

Live broker: A human being who answers calls and takes orders.

National Association of Securities Dealers (NASD): The American self-regulatory organization of the securities industry responsible for the regulation of Nasdaq and the over-the-counter markets.

Online broker: A brokerage firm that allows clients to trade over the Internet using Web-based trading platforms.

Options approval form: A document that must be completed by traders before trading options is allowed by a brokerage firm. Brokerage firms use the form in order to determine if options trading is suitable for the investor.

Options Clearing Corporation (OCC): The clearing entity for all U.S. options exchanges. The OCC is the guarantor and is responsible for ensuring that contracts are fulfilled.

Order: A customer request to buy or sell an investment security.

Payment for order flow: The practice of routing orders to specific exchanges in return for payments. Various brokerage firms engage in this controversial practice.

Privileged information: Information that is not available to the public. *See also* **Inside information** and **Insider trading**.

Retail investor: Individual investor making decisions for a personal portfolio. In contrast to institutional investors who make decisions on behalf of financial institutions, retail investors represent individual trading accounts.

Securities and Exchange Commission (SEC): A commission created by Congress to regulate the securities markets and protect investors. It is composed of five commissioners appointed by the President of the United States and approved by the Senate. The SEC enforces, among other acts, the Securities Act of 1933, the Securities Exchange Act of 1934, the Trust Indenture Act of 1939, the Investment Company Act of 1940, and the Investment Advisers Act of 1940.

Self-directed broker: A firm that caters to brokerage customers who make their own decisions and seek lower commissions.

Series 7: An examination for a license that allows individual stockbrokers to serve brokerage customers.

Ticket: The details of a trade—number of shares, type of order, prices—that must be submitted for a trade to be executed. In the past, this information was handwritten on a piece of paper called a ticket.

CHAPTER 13

Processing Your Trade

SUMMARY

Trades are executed on exchanges. This chapter explores the process that a trade goes through from beginning to end. Stocks, futures, and options trades are investigated in depth so that the reader can understand the extraordinary process a trade goes through to be executed. Additionally, it is essential to master the art of placing orders. This chapter also investigates the order process itself, including guiding the reader through this precise process.

There are many variables and terms that are used in the trading field. In addition, each broker has his or her own way of doing things. Nonetheless, by learning the basic concepts and being clear when placing an order, even a new trader can place a complicated trade correctly. Though most traders stick to using market and limit orders, it's a good idea to get a basic understanding of the various order-placing terms so that you are aware of what is available for you as a trader.

QUESTIONS AND EXERCISES

1. What are the three primary U.S. stock exchanges?

   1. ______________________________

   2. ______________________________

   3. ______________________________

2. U.S. exchanges are regulated by the _____________.
   A. U.S. Congress.
   B. National Stock Exchange Commission.
   C. Securities and Exchange Commission.
   D. Securities Exchange Act.

3. The _____________ regulates the nation's commodity futures exchanges.
   A. Commodity Futures Trading Commission.
   B. Securities and Exchange Commission.
   C. National Commodity Exchange Commission.
   D. U.S. Congress.

4. Describe the process your order goes through to get filled at a stock exchange.

   ____

   ____

5. A _____________ is there to create liquidity and narrow the spread.
   A. Specialist.
   B. Floor broker.
   C. Market maker.
   D. Exchange officer.

6. Orders are filled by a system of _____________ at a commodities exchange.
   A. Electronic review.
   B. Specialists making transaction matches.
   C. Market makers creating a market.
   D. Open outcry.

7. Floor traders make most of their money on _____________.
   A. The bid-ask spread.
   B. Commissions.
   C. Leasing their seats.
   D. All of the above.

8. The _____________ is the highest-volume stock options exchange.
   A. New York Stock Exchange (NYSE).
   B. Chicago Board Options Exchange (CBOE).
   C. American Stock Exchange (AMEX).
   D. Pacific Exchange (San Francisco).

9. A/an _____________ is an individual who is licensed to buy and sell marketplace securities and/or derivatives directly to traders and investors.
   A. Market maker.
   B. Speculator.
   C. Arbitrageur.
   D. Broker.

10. True or False: Someone who is licensed to take an order must have the knowledge to invest your money wisely.

11. Your broker—as your intermediary—will get paid a/an _____________ for each transaction.
    A. Round turn.
    B. Arbitrage.
    C. Commission.
    D. Dividend.

12. True or False: Never make an investment while on the phone with a sales call. End the call, and then think about what was told to you and do your own analysis of risk and reward.

13. A/an _____________ is the price that you are given on an executed trade.
    A. Buy.
    B. Bid.
    C. Ask.
    D. Fill.

14. Make a list of important items that need to be specified when placing an order.
    1. ____
    2. ____

3. ______________________________
4. ______________________________
5. ______________________________
6. ______________________________
7. ______________________________

15. If you place a ____________, you will get an immediate fill at the current price.

    A. Limit order.
    B. Market order.
    C. Day order.
    D. Stop order.

16. If you place a ____________, you will have to wait until the price you want gets hit before the broker can execute your trade.

    A. Limit order.
    B. Market order.
    C. Day order.
    D. Stop order.

17. You want to place the following market order: Short 100 Shares of IBM @ $87 and Long 2 September IBM 90 ATM Calls. What would you tell your broker?

    ____

    ____

18. The more volatile the market is, the ____________ the bid-ask spread will be.

    A. Narrower.
    B. Wider.
    C. More consistent.
    D. More fluctuating.

19. Floor prices primarily depend on ____________.

    A. Your broker's execution and the exchange.
    B. The bid-ask spread and volatility.
    C. The bid-ask spread and liquidity.
    D. Liquidity and volatility.

MEDIA ASSIGNMENT

In this chapter's media assignment, readers are encouraged to learn more about how options trades are processed by visiting the web sites of the key U.S. options exchanges. Today, there are six options exchanges in the United States. The two largest, the Chicago Board Options Exchange (CBOE) and the International Securities Exchange (ISE), handle the lion's share of the volume. However, all six exchanges have web sites available to investors. The web sites and addresses are as follows:

Chicago Board Options Exchange	www.cboe.com
The International Securities Exchange	www.iseoptions.com
The Boston Options Exchange	www.bostonoptions.com
The Philadelphia Stock Exchange	www.phlx.com
The American Stock Exchange	www.amex.com
The Pacific Stock Exchange	www.pacificex.com

Take a few minutes at each web site and look around. On the first stop at the Chicago Board Options Exchange web site, pay special attention to the "About CBOE" area of the site. Within this section, readers will find a history of the Chicago Board Options Exchange. Looking through the thirty-year history of the first organized options exchange gives great insight about the development and evolution of options trading in the United States.

On your next stop, the International Securities Exchange web site includes detailed descriptions of the technology that drives this relatively new options exchange. It also explains its current structure and membership information. Similarly, the Boston Options Exchange, which is the newest exchange, provides detailed descriptions about how this modern trading mechanism works day-in and day-out.

The remaining three options exchanges also have web sites. These exchanges trade both stocks and options. Therefore, readers can find information about the stocks and options traded on their web sites. For example, the "At the AMEX" section of the American Stock Exchange's web site includes information about the structure of the exchange as well as the trade execution process. Taken together, readers can find a wealth of information about how the options market works at the six web sites of the U.S. options exchanges, which will also help develop a good understanding about the options trading process.

VOCABULARY LIST

Exchange

Limit order

Market maker

Market order

Options Clearing Corporation (OCC)

Options Industry Council (OIC)

Specialist

SOLUTIONS

1. What are the three primary U.S. stock exchanges?

   Answer: New York Stock Exchange (NYSE), American Stock Exchange (AMEX), Nasdaq.

   Discussion: These are the main exchanges and the ones that we hear about the most on television and read about in the newspaper. However, there are many other exchanges that play a role in providing liquidity and opportunity for stock, options, and futures traders.

2. U.S. exchanges are regulated by the ____________.

   Answer: C—Securities and Exchange Commission.

   Discussion: The SEC has a major role in policing and setting up the appropriate rules and regulations for the marketplace. There have been several acts passed by Congress that the SEC has to enforce. There have been many high-profile cases the past five years that the SEC has had to oversee.

3. The ____________ regulates the nation's commodity futures exchanges.

   Answer: A—Commodity Futures Trading Commission.

   Discussion: Similar to the SEC, the CFTC regulates activity in the commodity exchanges. This commission was set up by the Commodity Futures Trading Commission Act of 1974 and is made up of five commissioners appointed by the U.S. President and approved by the Senate.

4. Describe the process your order goes through to get filled at a stock exchange.

   Answer: You call your broker, who passes your order along via Designated Order Turnaround (DOT) or by wire to a floor broker. DOT is an electronic system on the New York Stock Exchange that is used to send small orders directly to the specialists' posts on the trading floor. DOT bypasses floor brokers and speeds up the execution of small orders. If your order is sent by wire to a floor broker, he or she will immediately try to fill your order or take it directly to a specialist. If the specialist matches your order, you will receive a call from your broker with confirmation that your order has been executed.

Discussion: The amazing thing about the order process is the speed with which it happens. If a market order is placed, it takes just a few seconds to get confirmation of the fill. Technology has made the process extremely fast and efficient.

5. A ______________ is there to create liquidity and narrow the spread.

   Answer: C—Market maker.

   Discussion: A market maker plays an important role in the order placing process. Market makers take the opposite side of a trade when there isn't anyone else to take it. This means that traders can get filled on a stock at any time if they are willing to pay the going price.

6. Orders are filled by a system of ______________ at a commodities exchange.

   Answer: D—Open outcry.

   Discussion: We all have seen movies where floor traders are screaming and yelling and making hand signals. While this might seem very unorganized, the open outcry method has worked for decades and continues to be the system used at the commodities exchanges.

7. Floor traders make most of their money on ______________.

   Answer: A—The bid-ask spread.

   Discussion: New traders often ask why they can't buy at the bid and sell at the ask. This is because the floor traders need to make something for the services they offer. Just like a retail store, they are not going to sell something unless they can make a profit.

8. The ______________ is the highest-volume stock options exchange.

   Answer: B—Chicago Board Options Exchange (CBOE).

   Discussion: The CBOE was the first options exchange to be established (1973). Since that time, options volume has grown at an incredible rate. Although other options exchanges have been created, the CBOE remains the most popular.

9. A/an ______________ is an individual who is licensed to buy and sell marketplace securities and/or derivatives directly to traders and investors.

   Answer: D—Broker.

Discussion: A broker is the liaison between a trader and the exchanges. With the advent of online trading, hundreds of new companies have been established that offer brokerage services. The huge increase in the number of choices often makes it difficult to narrow down the universe of brokers to the few that you want to use.

10. True or False: Someone who is licensed to take an order must have the knowledge to invest your money wisely.

    Answer: False.

    Discussion: In any profession, just because you have a license to perform certain functions doesn't mean you are knowledgeable enough to make wise choices. This is why it is important to ask the appropriate questions when interviewing a new broker. The Optionetics site has an entire section dedicated to helping traders choose a broker, so use this to your advantage.

11. Your broker—as your intermediary—will get paid a/an ____________ for each transaction.

    Answer: C—Commission.

    Discussion: Commissions have come down substantially with the advent of the Internet. Even so, there still are various types of brokers, and their commissions vary widely depending on what services they offer. Online brokers charge small commissions if they do nothing other than route the trade. Full-service brokers charge considerably more per transaction because of the various services they offer.

12. True or False: Never make an investment while on the phone with a sales call. End the call, and then think about what was told to you and do your own analysis of risk and reward.

    Answer: True.

    Discussion: Individuals get sales calls all the time with the caller trying to sell various investments. However, it is important to do the appropriate research before investing in any stock or commodity. Don't be lured in by promises of riches and wealth. Though some of these investments might be worth a look, take the time to study the investment vehicle before committing your hard-earned cash.

13. A/an ____________ is the price that you are given on an executed trade.

    Answer: D—Fill.

    Discussion: After a trade has been entered, your broker will give you a fill price. The fill price could be the price at which a security was bought or sold. This initial price is the basis for figuring your profits and losses.

14. Make a list of important items that need to be specified when placing an order.

    Answer:

    1. What kind of order you wish to place.
    2. The exchange—where the order is to be placed (for futures and options).
    3. Quantity—number of contracts.
    4. Buy/sell—puts or calls (also include the strike price and expiration).
    5. Contract—name of the contract.
    6. Month—delivery month of the contract.
    7. Price—instructions regarding price execution.

    Discussion: Though a trader doesn't need to follow this exact format, it is a good idea to develop a system that works well for you and your broker. Generally, all of these components will need to be part of the order when placed on the phone. Even when using the Internet, it is a good idea to have this information written down to make sure no errors are made.

15. If you place a _____________, you will get an immediate fill at the current price.

    Answer: B—Market order.

    Discussion: Market orders are the best-known type of order and are used frequently when trading stock. However, an options trader should use limit orders to avoid getting filled at a price much different than expected. Market orders should be used only when a trader needs an immediate fill and is trading a highly liquid security.

16. If you place a _____________, you will have to wait until the price you want gets hit before the broker can execute your trade.

    Answer: A—Limit order.

    Discussion: Limit orders might take a longer time to fill, but they protect traders from getting a price they didn't want. Limit orders work well when trading options because liquidity on some options might not be high enough to use market orders.

17. You want to place the following market order: Short 100 Shares of IBM @ $87 and Long 2 September IBM 90 ATM Calls. What would you tell your broker?

    Answer: "I want to buy two September/Labor Day IBM at-the-money calls and sell 100 shares of IBM at the market."

Discussion: The term *Labor Day* is used to clarify that the month is September and not December. This isn't necessary, but it helps ensure that the broker understands the complete trade. The clearer you are, the better the chance that the trade will be filled correctly.

18. The more volatile the market is, the ____________ the bid-ask spread will be.

    Answer: B—Wider.

    Discussion: High volatility creates high risk for floor traders. Hence, the higher the risk to the floor trader, the higher the bid-ask spread will be. This is most notable when trading options because volume is much lighter for options than for most stocks.

19. Floor prices primarily depend on ____________.

    Answer: D—Liquidity and volatility.

    Discussion: Supply and demand play a major role in the prices for stocks and options. When there isn't much demand for a stock or option, the bid-ask spread will normally be wider. When volatility is high for a security, the bid-ask spread will be wider as well. This is why it is important to trade securities with liquidity.

MEDIA ASSIGNMENT

Today, six U.S. options exchanges compete for your trades. Some, like the Chicago Board Options Exchange and the American Stock Exchange, have been around for quite some time. Others, such as the Boston Options Exchange and the International Securities Exchange, are relatively new players on the scene. The two largest, which handle the majority of options volume today, are the Chicago Board Options Exchange and the International Securities Exchange.

All six options exchanges have excellent web sites. In this chapter, readers are encouraged to visit each one and pay special attention to the history of each exchange as well as the areas of the site that explain how each is designed or structured. Doing so provides better insight into the workings and flavor of each exchange, which will also help you to better understand how options trades are processed.

VOCABULARY DEFINITIONS

Exchange: Place where a stock or an option, a future, or other derivative is bought and sold. The best-known exchange is the New York Stock Exchange.

Limit order: An order to buy a stock at or below a specified price or to sell a stock at or above a specified price. For instance, you could tell a broker, "Buy me 100 shares of XYZ Corporation at $8 or less" or "Sell 100 shares of XYZ at $10 or better."

Market maker: A dealer willing to accept the risk of holding a particular security in his or her own account to facilitate trading in that security. On the over-the-counter markets, there are individuals and companies that maintain bids and offers for stocks. They must be prepared to buy or sell stocks from investors at any time.

Market order: An order to buy or sell securities at the price given at the time the order reaches the market. This can be different from the price on the broker's screen, depending on how fast the market is moving. A market order is to be executed immediately at the best available price, and is the only order that guarantees execution.

Options Clearing Corporation (OCC): Established in 1973, the organization processes and guarantees the standardized options contracts that trade on the U.S. options exchanges. It is the world's largest equity derivatives clearing organization.

Options Industry Council (OIC): A nonprofit association created to inform and educate investors about the benefits of listed options contracts. Formed in 1992, the OIC is sponsored by the major options exchanges and the Options Clearing Corporation (OCC).

Specialist: A stock exchange member who stands ready to quote and trade certain securities either for his or her own account or for customer accounts. The specialist's role is to maintain a fair and orderly market in the stocks for which he or she is responsible. A trader on the market floor is assigned to fill bids/orders in a specific stock out of his or her own account when the order has no competing bid/order to ensure a fair and orderly market.

CHAPTER 14

Margin and Risk

SUMMARY

Every investment or trade has a potential risk and a possible reward. Theoretically, the greater an investment's risk, the greater the potential reward. However, in the options market, it is possible to create trades that have relatively high rewards, but limited risk. In addition, some strategies have unlimited risks, but only modest rewards. By the conclusion of this book, the reader should understand this relationship and should be able to utilize strategies that minimize risk while maximizing potential rewards.

In this chapter, the basic concepts of risk and margin are explored. As we have duly noted, risk is inherent in every trade. There are ways to minimize it, but risk is always a factor to consider. For example, what is the risk of holding cash? Is there a risk? Yes, the risk of holding paper currency is that inflation will erode its purchasing power. So, regardless of the investment or strategy, risk is one of the most important characteristics of each investment's viability.

Meanwhile, margin, which is the amount of cash required to be on deposit with a trader's clearing firm in order to execute a trade, can also alter the reward/risk ratio. In this chapter, the reader will learn what margin is and how it works, as well as its key advantages and disadvantages.

QUESTIONS AND EXERCISES

1. What are the two key elements that characterize attractive trades?

   1. ______________________________

   2. ______________________________

2. What are the two most important factors in determining the cost of an investment?

   1. ______________________________

   2. ______________________________

3. A/an ______________ requires you to put up 100 percent of the money to execute the trade.

   A. Margin trade.
   B. Cash trade.
   C. Open trade.
   D. None of the above.

4. A/an ______________ allows you to put up a percentage of the calculated amount in cash and the rest is "on account."

   A. Margin trade.
   B. Cash trade.
   C. Open trade.
   D. None of the above.

5. ______________ is defined as the amount of cash required to be on deposit with your clearing firm to secure the integrity of the trade.

   A. Deposit.
   B. Commission.
   C. Adjustment.
   D. Margin.

6. A/an _____________ allows traders and investors to leverage their assets to produce a higher return.
   A. Cash account.
   B. Margin account.
   C. Absorption account.
   D. Adjunct account.

7. Margin accounts allow traders to extract up to _____________ of the cash value of their securities.
   A. 25 percent.
   B. 50 percent.
   C. 75 percent.
   D. 100 percent.

8. Using a margin account, if you buy 500 shares of XYZ at $100, how much will this trade cost you, not including commissions?
   A. $10,000.
   B. $20,000.
   C. $25,000.
   D. $50,000.

9. A _____________ from your broker requires you to place additional funds in your account. If you do not place these additional funds in your account, your position will be liquidated.
   A. Margin ratio.
   B. Margin account.
   C. Margin requirement.
   D. Margin call.

10. True or False: If you are trading delta neutral using futures and options, your margin will be close to zero, which means you will never get a margin call.

11. If the _____________ of your trade increases, then the margin will also increase.
    A. Implied risk.
    B. Risk premium.

C. Risk arbitrage.

D. Perceived risk.

12. If you do not have additional funds to place in your account to cover a margin call, your position will be ______________.
    A. Placed on hold.
    B. Liquidated.
    C. Traded by the brokerage firm.
    D. None of the above.

13. Based on the rules of the Securities and Exchange Commission and the clearing firms, margin for stocks equals ______________ of the amount of the trade.
    A. 25 percent.
    B. 35 percent.
    C. 50 percent.
    D. 75 percent.

14. For stock options, each point equals ______________.
    A. $10.
    B. $100.
    C. $500.
    D. An amount that depends on the stock.

15. Selling ______________ options, or placing an unprotected trade, has the highest risk and the highest margin requirements.
    A. Naked.
    B. Call.
    C. Put.
    D. Covered.

16. Combining the buying and selling of options, stocks, and/or futures creates a more complex calculation; however, this will ______________ your margin requirements.
    A. Increase.
    B. Decrease.
    C. Not affect.
    D. None of the above.

17. ______________ is the ability to use less capital for a larger potential return but can result in increased risk.
    A. Volatility.
    B. Liquidity.
    C. Flexibility.
    D. Leverage.

MEDIA ASSIGNMENT

The next media assignment takes a closer look at margin and margin accounts. When investors use margin, they deposit a percentage (normally 50 percent) of the cost of the investment security and borrow the rest. The brokerage charges the investor interest on the money borrowed. The advantage to buying stocks on margin, however, is that it enables the trader to control a greater amount of an investment with less capital. Therefore, margin equals leverage.

To learn more about margin accounts and current trends related to margin, let's visit the web site of the National Association of Securities Dealers (NASD). The home page is www.nasd.com. From there, click the "Investor Information" tab. Then choose "Markets & Trading" at the top of the page. Finally, click "Margin Information."

Once inside the Margin Information section of the National Association of Securities Dealers web site, readers will find a wealth of information related to this topic. A section called *Understanding Margin Accounts* walks the reader through real world examples and situations dealing with customer margin accounts. The *Purchasing on Margin* section discusses the potential risks of using margin. Current and historic levels of margin debt can be found in the *Margin Statistics* area of the site. The information at the NASD site offers traders the opportunity to gain a comprehensive understanding of margin including its potential benefits and pitfalls.

VOCABULARY LIST

Cash account
Cash trade
Federal Reserve
Leverage
Liquidation
Margin
Margin account
Margin call
Margin debt
Margin requirement
Margin trade
Marginable security
Naked writing
Risk

SOLUTIONS

1. What are the two key elements that characterize attractive trades?

   Answer: Limited risk and unlimited reward.

   Discussion: Worthwhile options trades put a limit on possible losses, but also offer the potential for large rewards. Trades that possess the opposite characteristics (i.e., unlimited risks and limited rewards) are generally discouraged.

2. What are the two most important factors in determining the cost of an investment?

   Answer: The size of the transaction (number of shares, futures, or options) and the risk calculated on the trade.

   Discussion: The cost of a trade has two components. First, what is the cash outlay in terms of the number of shares/contracts times the market prices? Second, what is the possible loss or risk of the trade? Sometimes these two costs can differ significantly.

3. A/an ______________ requires you to put up 100 percent of the money to execute the trade.

   Answer: B—Cash trade.

   Discussion: In a cash trade, the investor is required to pay 100 percent of the cost of the trade. Since options cannot be purchased on margin, buying puts and calls is an example of a cash trade.

4. A/an ______________ allows you to put up a percentage of the calculated amount in cash and the rest is "on account."

   Answer: A—Margin trade.

   Discussion: In a margin account, traders can buy stocks for less than the 100 percent required to cover the cost of the trade. For instance, stock traders using margin accounts can buy stocks for 50 percent of the actual cost of the trade. Margin requirements can change over time, however.

5. ______________ is defined as the amount of cash required to be on deposit with your clearing firm to secure the integrity of the trade.

   Answer: D—Margin.

   Discussion: Margin is the amount of money you are required to post to secure a position and the amount a company will lend you against the security of the investment you seek to buy.

6. A/an ____________ allows traders and investors to leverage their assets to produce a higher return.

   Answer: B—Margin account.

   Discussion: To buy and sell securities using margin, the client must first open a margin account with a brokerage firm.

7. Margin accounts allow traders to extract up to ____________ of the cash value of their securities.

   Answer: B—50 percent.

   Discussion: Currently, the margin requirements are 50 percent. However, margin requirements can change over time, so investors should check with their brokerage firms periodically before initiating margin trades.

8. Using a margin account, if you buy 500 shares of XYZ at $100, how much will this trade cost you, not including commissions?

   Answer: C—$25,000.

   Discussion: Buying 500 shares of XYZ at $100 a share would cost $50,000. Since the margin requirement is 50 percent, or half, the trader pays $25,000 for 500 shares if the stock is purchased on margin.

9. A ____________ from your broker requires you to place additional funds in your account. If you do not place these additional funds in your account, your positions will be liquidated.

   Answer: D—Margin call.

   Discussion: A margin call occurs if the equity value in a margin account drops below a certain level. The deposit into the account must occur within one business day. If not, securities in the account will probably be sold to cover the margin call.

10. True or False: If you are trading delta neutral using futures and options, your margin will be close to zero, which means you will never get a margin call.

    Answer: False.

    Discussion: If your futures side starts losing money, you may get a margin call.

11. If the ____________ of your trade increases, then the margin will also increase.

    Answer: D—Perceived risk.

    Discussion: Higher risk strategies, like naked call selling, have higher margin requirements. The exact dollar amount will vary from one brokerage firm to the next.

12. If you do not have additional funds to place in your account to cover a margin call, your position will be ____________.

    Answer: B—Liquidated.

    Discussion: In order to cover a margin call, an investor must either add more cash to the account or liquidate some of the holdings within the account. The amount that is liquidated will depend on the amount needed to cover the margin call.

13. Based on the rules of the Securities and Exchange Commission and the clearing firms, margin for stocks equals ____________ of the amount of the trade.

    Answer: C—50 percent.

    Discussion: Current margin requirements are 50 percent, but are occasionally subject to change.

14. For stock options, each point of the premium equals ____________.

    Answer: B—$100.

    Discussion: The multiplier for stock options is 100. So an options contract trading for a premium of 1 is worth $100 a contract.

15. Selling ____________ options, or placing an unprotected trade, has the highest risk and the highest margin requirements.

    Answer: A—Naked.

    Discussion: Naked options writing carries extremely high risk. As a result, brokerage firms impose high margin requirements for this type of trading activity.

16. Combining the buying and selling of options, stocks, and/or futures creates a more complex calculation; however, this will _______________ your margin requirements.

    Answer: B—Decrease.

    Discussion: In general, more complex strategies that involve buying and selling options as well as the underlying instrument can reduce the overall risk of the trade. Consequently, the margin requirements should be less. However, the margin requirements for complex trades will often vary among brokerage firms.

17. _______________ is the ability to use less capital for a larger potential return but can result in increased risk.

    Answer: D—Leverage.

    Discussion: In the financial markets, leverage is using small amounts of money to control a much larger position. Stock options are an example of leverage because by paying a small premium investors can control a large number of shares.

MEDIA ASSIGNMENT

Margin is a double-edged sword. While it can be used as leverage to generate higher returns, the effect of added leverage can also lead to greater losses. Hence, the decision to use margin is ultimately left to the whim of the individual trader. Basically, margin results in a higher risk-reward situation. The decision to use margin is an important one and therefore deserves careful consideration.

In order to better understand the possible benefits and potential pitfalls of using margin, readers are encouraged to visit the "Margin Information" section of the NASD web site. It probably offers the most comprehensive look at margin available anywhere. Real world examples and situations help to understand exactly how margin accounts work. In addition, readers will find the latest margin statistics, information on purchasing on margin, as well as potential risks associated with margin trading.

As you can see, leverage will have a significant effect on the risk-reward outlook when 50 percent margin is used to buy shares. For instance, a 25 percent decline in the stock price results in a 50 percent loss in the margin account. However, a 10 percent gain in the stock translates into a 20 percent gain using 50 percent margin. So, the risks are greater and the rewards potential is also higher when investors use margin to buy stocks.

VOCABULARY DEFINITIONS

Cash account: A type of brokerage account that requires investors to pay for trades in their entirety, which is in contrast to a margin account that allows customers to use collateral to buy securities.

Cash trade: A trade that must be paid for in its entirety once it is initiated.

Federal Reserve: The U.S. central bank that is responsible for monetary policy. The Federal Reserve will change interest rates and the money supply in an effort to keep the economy expanding at a reasonable pace.

Leverage: Using a small amount of capital to control a much larger amount of capital. Options are an example of a trading instrument that offers a high leverage trading approach.

Liquidation: When the assets within a portfolio are sold or cashed out.

Margin: A deposit made by a trader with a clearinghouse to ensure that he/she will fulfill any financial obligations resulting from his or her trades. Margin is the amount of money a company will lend you against the security of the investment you buy.

Margin account: An account in which stocks can be purchased for a combination of cash and a loan. The loan in the margin account is collateralized by the stock, and if the value of the stock drops sufficiently, the owner will be asked to either put in more cash or sell a portion of the stock.

Margin call: The brokerage's demand that a customer deposit a specified amount of money or securities when a purchase is made in a margin account; the amount is expressed as a percentage of the market value of the securities at the time of purchase. The deposit must be made within one payment period.

Margin debt: The total amount of money that has been borrowed from brokers to pay for margin trades.

Margin requirement: The amount of cash an uncovered (naked) option writer is required to deposit and maintain to cover the daily position valuation and reasonably foreseeable intraday price changes.

Margin trade: A trade that is executed in a margin account using less than 100 percent cash to pay for the transaction.

Marginable security: An investment that can be used as collateral in a margin account. A brokerage firm can tell you whether your investment is marginable. Most exchange-traded stocks are, but options contracts are not.

Naked writing: Selling options with no hedge or offsetting position.

Risk: The potential loss associated with a trade or investment.

CHAPTER 15

A Short Course in Economic Analyses

SUMMARY

Economists don't often make good traders, but having a basic understanding of economic trends can help make sense of the day-to-day happenings in the futures, bond, and stock markets. For instance, an economic report can cause bond prices to tumble, interest rates to shoot higher, and stock index futures to fall. When the moves are sudden and short-term in nature, they can cause volatility in the stock market to spike higher. However, long periods of stable or falling interest rates can keep volatility at bay and create a favorable environment for higher stock prices.

This chapter explores the relationships between interest rates, bond prices, and stocks. An important factor to keep in mind is that when interest rates move higher, bond prices tumble. And when rates fall, bonds rally. In addition, sudden jumps in interest rates can cause money to shift out of stocks and into interest-bearing investments—which can also make prices fall in the stock market. However, when interest rates are low, investors are more inclined to look for profits in the stock market, and that trend can help lift share prices over the long term. In sum, for those readers interested in trading stock index options, index futures, and even shares of large companies, this chapter is designed to help you by providing a short course in economic analysis.

QUESTIONS AND EXERCISES

1. The ______________ has a corresponding futures contract that is traded at the Chicago Board of Trade (CBOT) and reflects one very important aspect of many people's lives: mortgage interest rates.
   A. S&P 500.
   B. OEX.
   C. Ten-year note.
   D. Crude oil.

2. In a typical situation, if interest rates go up, bond prices ______________.
   A. Go up.
   B. Go down.
   C. Stay the same.
   D. Go either way—you can never really tell.

3. Bond prices and the stock market should ______________.
   A. Go in the same direction.
   B. Have an inverse relationship.
   C. Go in opposite directions.
   D. Have no relationship whatsoever.

4. If interest rates go sideways, stock prices will probably ______________.
   A. Rise.
   B. Fall.
   C. Go sideways.
   D. Rise at first and then fall steadily.

5. There are periods when a/an ______________ occurs and stock prices rise regardless of whether interest rates go up or down.
   A. Inverse relationship.
   B. Contrarian effect.
   C. Divergence.
   D. Momentum push.

6. If you see interest rates ______________ quickly, you don't want to be a buyer of stocks.
   A. Increasing.
   B. Decreasing.
   C. Increasing sharply and then falling off.
   D. Decreasing slowly and then rising.

7. If you find that interest rates are ______________, being a buyer of stocks is a good idea because the stock market will have an upward bias.
   A. Increasing.
   B. Decreasing.
   C. Stable or increasing.
   D. Stable or decreasing.

MEDIA ASSIGNMENT

In order to better understand economic events, let's begin tuning in to the happenings in the bond market. One of the best ways to do this is to watch financial TV news before the start of stock trading. The bond market opens and closes one hour before the stock market, so bonds begin trading at 8:30 A.M. New York time. Furthermore, since many economic reports are released before the start of stock trading, the bond market will often react to news first.

So, at 8:30 A.M. Eastern time (that's 5:30 A.M. for West Coast traders), turn on CNBC and Bloomberg news and look for their reports that come from the Chicago Board of Trade (CBOT). At the time of this writing, CNBC offers live coverage of the start of trading on the CBOT every weekday morning one hour before the start of stock trading. The report summarizes the important daily economic news, forthcoming economic reports, and many other economic events (changes in oil prices, changes in interest rates, activity in the currency markets) that can have an impact on both stocks and bonds.

VOCABULARY LIST

Bond
Bond trader
Chicago Board of Trade (CBOT)
Correlation
Economist
Fed funds rate
Interest rate
Interest-bearing security
Inverse relationship
Maturity
Treasury bill
Treasury bond
Treasury note
Yield

SOLUTIONS

1. The ______________ has a corresponding futures contract that is traded at the Chicago Board of Trade (CBOT) and reflects one very important aspect of many people's lives: mortgage interest rates.

   Answer: C—Ten-year note.

   Discussion: The Treasury's 10-year note has become a barometer for the performance of the bond market. This bond is actively traded and has a futures contract trading on the CBOT. As this futures contract moves higher, it indicates that bond traders expect that interest rates, which move opposite to the note, will fall going forward. When the 10-year note futures contract falls, it is a sign that bond traders expect rates to rise. As rates rise and fall, the long-term trend can impact many aspects of people's lives, including mortgage rates.

2. In a typical situation, if interest rates go up, bond prices ______________.

   Answer: B—Go down.

   Discussion: Bond prices move opposite to yields or rates. As bond prices fall, rates start moving higher.

3. Bond prices and the stock market should ______________.

   Answer: A—Go in the same direction.

   Discussion: In general, bond prices will move in the same direction as stock prices because falling interest rates often bode well for both stocks and bonds. Rising interest rates are considered a negative for stocks and bonds, so if rates experience a sudden move higher, stocks and bonds tend to fall.

4. If interest rates go sideways, stock prices will probably _______________.

   Answer: A—Rise.

   Discussion: Over the long haul, the path of least resistance for stocks is to move higher. So, if interest rates are not a factor, stocks will probably head higher.

5. There are periods when a/an _______________ occurs and stock prices rise regardless of whether interest rates go up or down.

   Answer: C—Divergence.

   Discussion: Company earnings can continue to improve, pushing stock prices up, even if interest rates move higher. In this case, a divergence might occur, with stocks rising and bonds falling.

6. If you see interest rates _______________ quickly, you don't want to be a buyer of stocks.

   Answer: A—Increasing.

   Discussion: Sudden spikes in interest rates often spook investors in the stock market. Interest-bearing securities like bonds and savings accounts become more competitive compared to stocks. At the same time, higher rates can make stock prices seem more expensive when using various valuation models.

7. If you find that interest rates are _______________, being a buyer of stocks is a good idea because the stock market will have an upward bias.

   Answer: D—Stable or decreasing.

   Discussion: Long-term periods of stable or falling interest rates often provide a favorable environment for higher stock prices. Lower rates make money more readily available for borrowing, investing, and building successful businesses. At the same time, interest-bearing investments become less attractive compared to stocks when rates fall.

MEDIA ASSIGNMENT

If you have been watching the early morning news reports from the financial news services like CNBC and Bloomberg TV, you have probably noticed that trading in the bond market can become quite chaotic at times. Traders in the bond pits are continually trying to assess if interest rates are going to move higher or lower, and then buying and selling based on those expectations. In addition, since so many factors can influence interest rates (economic news, geopolitical unrest, oil prices, fluctuations in the currency markets, stock prices, etc.), bond traders have a great deal of information to digest.

Yet, while trading in the bond pits can turn frantic, the long-term relationship between stock prices and bonds is fairly clear. Specifically, periods of long-term bond strength and falling yields are generally bullish for stocks. Conversely, when interest rates are expected to move sharply higher, stocks have a tendency to move lower and experience greater volatility. So changes in interest rates can be important to an options trader because longer-term trends can have an impact on both stock prices and overall levels of market volatility.

VOCABULARY DEFINITIONS

Bond: A debt obligation issued by a government (i.e., Treasury bond) or corporation (i.e., corporate bond) that promises to pay its bondholders periodic interest at a fixed rate (the coupon) and to repay the principal of the loan at maturity (a specified future date). Bonds are usually issued with a par or face value of $1,000, representing the principal or amount of money borrowed. The interest payment is stated on the face of the bond at issue.

Bond trader: An individual who works for a firm and buys and sells bonds for clients. Bond traders work via computers or in the trading pits of the Chicago Board of Trade.

Chicago Board of Trade (CBOT): The oldest commodity exchange in the United States, established in 1886. The exchange lists agricultural commodity futures such as corn, oats, and soybeans, in addition to more recent innovations such as financial futures.

Correlation: The relationship between the prices of two or more investments. For instance, if X moves higher and B moves lower, X and B have a negative correlation. If two assets move in the same direction, they have a positive correlation.

Economist: Generally, a paid professional, often with a doctorate degree, who makes forecasts regarding the economy, interest rates, and economic activity.

Federal funds rate: The short-term interest rate controlled by the Federal Reserve. The Federal Reserve will change this interest rate to stimulate or cool down the economy.

Interest rate: The cost of borrowing money.

Interest-bearing security: A type of investment on which earnings bear interest. Examples include money markets, certificates of deposit, and savings accounts.

Inverse relationship: When the prices of two assets move opposite to one another.

Maturity: The date on which a bond's principal is repaid to the investor and interest payments cease. Maturity is the number of years until the principal amount of a bond is due and payable by the issuer to its bondholders.

Treasury bill: Short-term government obligation that matures in 90 days or less.

Treasury bond: Long-term government obligation that has a maturity of up to 30 years.

Treasury note: Government obligation with 5 to 10 years until maturity.

Yield: Refers to the annual interest on a bond divided by the market price of that bond. The current yield is the actual income rate of return as opposed to the coupon rate or the yield to maturity.

CHAPTER 16

Mastering the Market

SUMMARY

This chapter offers guidelines and suggestions to enhance a trader's ability to find profitable trades. It introduces several concepts including low risk, time requirements, and risk tolerance as well as casting a glance at risk profiles and investment criteria. In order to become successful, traders need to figure out their own risk tolerance. Some of this has to do with the amount of capital available, and part has to do with time and stress. Nonetheless, every trade should consist of a high reward-to-risk ratio, resulting in a high probability of success.

Another part of successful trading has to do with money management and setting up the appropriate system. Since emotions play a huge part in trading, traders are encouraged to avoid emotional trading. Fear and greed move the markets, but good traders stick to their plans, using preset exit points. Exit strategies include time exits, profit exits, and loss exits. It is very difficult to rid yourself of emotion when trading, but by understanding your exits and goals in advance, you can gain control of this detriment to trading success.

Ultimately, you need to rely on your own knowledge and research to become a successful trader. Many who have relied on analyst comments and advice from self-proclaimed gurus have ultimately found failure. There are many companies available to help you learn the rules of trading, including Optionetics, but ultimately it is up to you to do the research necessary and to enter and exit a trade correctly.

QUESTIONS AND EXERCISES

1. Name as many elements of a good investment as you can.

   ____

   ____

   ____

   ____

2. ____________ of any investment must take into account the following elements: potential risk, potential reward, the probability of success, and how long the investment takes to make a return.
   A. Limiting the risk.
   B. The reward/risk ratio.
   C. The delta neutrality.
   D. All of the above.

3. Studying a risk profile can show you the potential increasing or decreasing profit and loss of a trade relative to the underlying asset's ____________ over a specific period of time.
   A. Volatility.
   B. Volume.
   C. Price.
   D. Change in direction.

4. The best investments will have an opportunity for ____________ with acceptable risk and a high probability of winning on a consistent basis.
   A. High reward.
   B. High volatility.
   C. High liquidity.
   D. Major market movement.

5. True or False: If you do not have the time to sit in front of a computer day in, day out, then your best investments will be day trades.

6. Your risk tolerance level is directly proportional to your ____________.
   A. Knowledge of the markets.
   B. Computer availability.

C. Time requirements.
D. Available investment capital.

7. Name a few investment objectives.

____

____

MEDIA ASSIGNMENT

This chapter discusses risk tolerance and how to take emotion out of trading. Having a set plan in advance for entering a trade is an important key to lowering the part emotions play in our trading success. If traders take risks that do not fit their risk tolerance, this will increase the emotions felt while trading. For this media assignment, take the time to write down your risk tolerance and goals. This includes writing down the time you have available to trade, the amount of capital that will be used to trade, and the profit goals you have set for your trading account. From the first trade, keep a trading journal that tracks not only the details of each trade, but the emotions and feelings you had as the trade progressed. You'll be amazed at how much knowledge can be gleaned from reading the information found in a trading journal.

VOCABULARY LIST

Bear market
Bull market
Capital
Capital gains
Interest income
Price/earnings (P/E) ratio

SOLUTIONS

1. Name as many elements of a good investment as you can.

   Answer: A good investment has low risk, a favorable risk profile, and high potential return. It meets your time constraints, risk tolerance level, and investment criteria. It also meets your investment capital constraints and can be easily understood.

Discussion: This might seem like a lot to remember, but it all makes sense. However, it is amazing how often new traders enter trades that have horrible risk profiles or that don't meet their time constraints. Initially, a new trader might need to go through each of these criteria to make sure a trade makes sense. After a while, this type of analysis will become second nature, allowing a trader to make healthy profits, even while limiting risk.

2. ____________ of any investment must take into account the following elements: potential risk, potential reward, the probability of success, and how long the investment takes to make a return.

   Answer: B—The reward/risk ratio.

   Discussion: All traders want to make as much profit as possible with the capital used in their trades. By looking at a risk graph, many of the problems with a trade can be uncovered. The reward/risk ratio can help you to determine the validity of a trade. However, you also need to understand the probability of success and how long the reward will take to accumulate, in addition to the basic risks and rewards possible.

3. Studying a risk profile can show you the potential increasing or decreasing profit and loss of a trade relative to the underlying asset's ____________ over a specific period of time.

   Answer: C—Price.

   Discussion: A risk graph helps a trader view how the trade will change in value given a move in the underlying security's price. Of course, there are other variables that can impact an option's value, but the main component is the price of the underlying. It is easy to create a risk graph for simple strategies like long calls and long puts, but more complicated strategies might require the use of a computer program to view a correct risk graph.

4. The best investments will have an opportunity for ____________ with acceptable risk and a high probability of winning on a consistent basis.

   Answer: A—High reward.

   Discussion: It wouldn't make sense for a trader to enter a trade that has a loss potential of $5,000 when the maximum reward is just $1,000—that is, unless the probability of success is very high. This is the very reason why we do not suggest naked option strategies, as these trades are extremely high risk and offer only a small reward. Though they have a high probability of success in most cases, the one time when the trade goes against you can ruin your entire trading account.

5. True or False: If you do not have the time to sit in front of a computer day in, day out, then your best investments will be day trades.

   Answer: False.

   Discussion: Day trading requires the attention of a trader on a minute-by-minute basis. This obviously wouldn't be appropriate for a professional who trades only occasionally. Before entering a trade, a trader should look at the time needed to manage the trade. If this time commitment can't be made, move on to a trade that can be handled in the time you have available.

6. Your risk tolerance level is directly proportional to your ______________.

   Answer: D – Available investment capital.

   Discussion: Though there are traders with large accounts who have very low risk tolerances, normally the amount of capital available is the largest determinant for a trader's risk tolerance. When trading options and individual stocks and futures, we should never use money we can't afford to lose. Though we don't plan on losing the money, if we can't afford to lose it our emotions will take control of our trading.

7. Name a few investment objectives.

   Answer: Interest income, tax-free government securities, capital gains.

   Discussion: Most traders view their main investing objective as making money. However, this has many meanings depending on the trader and his or her situation in life. Older individuals who are in retirement might be concentrating mainly on income. Others might have tax problems that require a large amount of money to be placed in government securities. Even traders looking for capital gains should have an understanding of how their trades will be impacted by taxes.

MEDIA ASSIGNMENT

Setting up a trading journal will be a real eye-opener. By reading back through your thoughts and feelings during a trade, you'll learn a lot about your state of mind and how controlled you may be by emotion. Not only should you keep track of the details of a trade, but write down these feelings and review them consistently. By looking back on past trades, you can gain a better understanding of what you did right and what went wrong.

VOCABULARY DEFINITIONS

Bear market: A declining stock market over a prolonged period, usually lasting at least six months and normally not more than 18 months. Usually caused by a conviction that a weak economy will produce depressed corporate profits. Also, a market in which prices of a certain group of securities are falling or are expected to fall.

Bull market: A rising stock market over a prolonged period, usually lasting at least six months and normally not more than 18 months. Usually caused by a conviction that a strong economy will produce increased corporate profits. Also, a market in which prices of a certain group of securities are rising or are expected to rise.

Capital: The amount of money you have invested. When your investing objective is capital preservation, your priority is to try not to lose any money. When your objective is capital growth, your priority is to try to make your initial investment grow in value. Capital also refers to accumulated money or goods available for use in producing more money or goods.

Capital gains: The profit realized when a capital asset is sold for a higher price than the purchase price. Your costs (when you buy) include the commission you paid your broker and are deducted from the proceeds when you sell.

Interest income: A type of income generated from interest-bearing securities. The closer to retirement a person gets, the more important interest income usually becomes. Government bonds and high-dividend-paying stocks provide this type of income.

Price-earnings (P/E) ratio: A tool for comparing the prices of different common stocks by assessing how much the market is willing to pay for a share of each corporation's earnings. It is calculated by dividing the current market price of a stock by the earnings per share.

CHAPTER 17

How to Spot Explosive Opportunities

SUMMARY

No two traders are exactly alike. Some, like stock investors, spend a lot of time studying individual companies, earnings reports, or financial statements. Others, like currency traders, are more focused on economic trends, interest rates, and geopolitical events. Still others, such as futures traders, are often more focused on charts and graphs. One method is not better than any other, but you will find that many successful traders specialize in one approach and become experts in that particular field of study.

In this chapter, the reader is introduced to a wide variety of methods—including fundamental, technical, and sentiment analysis—that can be used to help locate profitable trading opportunities. Readers are also encouraged to use various media sources, including *The Wall Street Journal*, *Investor's Business Daily*, and CNBC. In addition, a few informal techniques—from using the contrarian approach to critiquing products you own, as well as some effective stock indicators—are explored.

QUESTIONS AND EXERCISES

1. What are the two general forms of market analysis?

   1. ______________________________

   2. ______________________________

2. ______________ analysis is primarily concerned with the underlying factors of supply and demand regarding a stock or commodity.
   A. Fundamental.
   B. Technical.
   C. Sentiment.

3. Name some factors of fundamental analysis.

   ____

   ____

4. ______________ analysis is primarily concerned with statistics generated by market activity and the resulting patterns and trends.
   A. Fundamental.
   B. Technical.
   C. Sentiment.

5. Name two common tools of technical analysis.
   1. ____
   2. ____

6. ______________, probably the simplest and most widely used technical tool, calculate price action over a specified period of time as a mean or average.
   A. Technical charts.
   B. Moving averages.
   C. Momentum indicators.
   D. Contrarian approaches.

7. A ______________ utilizes price and volume statistics for predicting the strength or weakness of a current market and any overbought or oversold conditions.
   A. Technical chart.
   B. Moving average.
   C. Momentum indicator.
   D. Contrarian approach.

8. _____________ analysis is primarily concerned with the nature and impact of crowd psychology on financial markets.

   A. Fundamental.

   B. Technical.

   C. Sentiment.

9. Name some tools of sentiment analysis.

   ____

   ____

10. If you use _____________, you will be trading against the majority view of the marketplace.

    A. Charting techniques.

    B. Moving averages.

    C. Momentum indicators.

    D. The contrarian approach.

11. True or False: Fundamental and technical analysis are mutually exclusive—traders should learn to use one or the other.

12. By studying the daily reactions of specific markets to _____________, you can begin to forecast which strategy can be used to make the largest potential profit.

    A. Interest rates.

    B. Seasonal changes.

    C. Government reports.

    D. All of the above.

13. Name three ways you can spot potentially profitable investments when shopping in a retail store.

    1. ____

    2. ____

    3. ____

14. Name four ways to spot potential investments in your everyday life.

    1. ____

    2. ____

3. ____
4. ____

15. Data service providers can relay information in which three ways?
    1. ____
    2. ____
    3. ____

16. True or False: If you are going to sit in front of a computer all day long, then you don't really need real-time feeds.

17. ____________ was born from the Financial News Network (FNN), which was watched widely by the investment community.
    A. CNN Business.
    B. CNBC.
    C. CBS.
    D. FOX.

18. The best investments have ____________, which should be monitored over both a short and a long period of time.
    A. Cheap options.
    B. Low margin.
    C. Momentum.
    D. Low volatility.

19. An increase in a stock's ____________ signals movement and a good opportunity for investment.
    A. Price.
    B. Volume.
    C. Perceived risk.
    D. All of the above.

20. The best investments have a reasonable ____________ relative to the industry average.
    A. Settle.
    B. Yield and percent.
    C. P/E.
    D. Open interest.

21. Name six ways to spot potential profit-making stock opportunities.
    1. ______________________________
    2. ______________________________
    3. ______________________________
    4. ______________________________
    5. ______________________________
    6. ______________________________

22. A low-priced market trades for less than ____________.
    A. $10.
    B. $20.
    C. $30.
    D. $50.

23. Why is it easier to make money on low-priced markets?
    A. You can make a high return much faster.
    B. You have less invested to lose.
    C. You can play more stocks with less money.
    D. All of the above.

24. The theory behind ____________, the basis of a mutual fund, is that a larger group of stocks will even out the chances of winning in the long run.
    A. Diversification.
    B. A broad portfolio.
    C. Both A and B.
    D. None of the above.

25. Momentum investors are much more ____________ oriented than mutual fund investors or money managers.
    A. Short-term.
    B. Long-term.
    C. Volatility.
    D. Profit.

26. A long-term indicator of momentum can be measured by looking for a change in price of a stock over the previous ____________.
    A. 15 days.
    B. 30 days.
    C. 60 days.
    D. 90 days.
    E. Both A and B.
    F. Both C and D.

27. If a stock has increased or decreased in price more than ____________ since yesterday, this can be used to indicate a momentum investment.
    A. 5 percent.
    B. 10 percent.
    C. 15 percent.
    D. 20 percent.

28. If a stock trades less than ____________ shares daily, try to avoid it in short-term trading.
    A. 100,000.
    B. 300,000.
    C. 500,000.
    D. 1,000,000.

29. To apply the contrarian approach, look at the ____________ list to find stocks that have made major moves down (50 percent or greater) and then look for a rebound.
    A. Price Percentage Gainers.
    B. Price Percentage Losers.
    C. Volume Percentage Leaders.
    D. Lifetime High and Low.

30. The blow-off bottom may have occurred when a stock is coming off a new ____________.
    A. High price with high volume.
    B. High price with low volume.
    C. Low price with high volume.
    D. Low price with low volume.

MEDIA ASSIGNMENT

The purpose of this media assignment is to find a reliable source for stock charts and indicators. There are a number of ways to do so. A number of web sites offer stock charting capabilities—including the Interactive Wall Street Journal, Bloomberg.com, Stockcharts.com, BigCharts.com, Optionetics.com, and a host of others. If you have a brokerage account, your firm might also offer real-time charts. Subscriptions to more advanced charting programs such as TradeStation, eSignal, and ProfitSource sometimes make sense for more active traders who are looking for more sophisticated charting tools.

Whether using free trading capabilities online or using a more sophisticated software package, readers will want to begin reviewing charts on a regular basis. The first step is to select a small number of stocks that are actively traded. Look at the graphs over different time frames—daily, weekly, monthly. Understand that a trend can easily go from an uptrend to a downtrend depending on the time frame used in a chart. For example, what appears to be an uptrend on a daily chart could well be a downtrend on the monthly chart.

Next, apply indicators. Some important indicators have been discussed throughout the chapter. Moving average convergence/divergence (MACD), Bollinger bands, and Elliott Wave analysis are examples of common indicators that can be applied to charts using almost any software program or web-based charting tools. Look at a number of different stocks and consider how various indicators can help identify turning points in different situations. In conclusion, readers should begin charting stocks and applying indicators. Doing so provides a quick and easy way to see the price action and technical trends of a stock or index.

VOCABULARY LIST

Bar chart

Blow-off bottom

Blow-off top

Capitulation

Contrarian

Data feed

Diversification

Fund manager

Fundamental analysis

Momentum

Moving average

Moving average convergence/divergence (MACD)

Mutual fund

On balance volume (OBV)

Price-to-earnings ratio (P/E)

Real-time data

Seasonal patterns

Sentiment analysis

Technical analysis

Volume

SOLUTIONS

1. What are the two general forms of market analysis?

   Answer: Fundamental analysis and technical analysis.

   Discussion: Technical analysts rely heavily on charts, volume information, and trends. Fundamental analysts are more concerned with the company or the industry. So, instead of looking at charts, the fundamental analysts will spend more time with news releases, earnings reports, and other financial statements.

2. ____________ analysis is primarily concerned with the underlying factors of supply and demand regarding a stock or commodity.

   Answer: B—Technical.

   Discussion: Technical analysts will look at a chart along with volume information to study the balance of supply and demand with respect to a specific stock or commodity. Technical analysis is based on the theory that market prices display repetitive patterns that can be tracked and used to forecast future price movement.

3. Name some factors of fundamental analysis.

   Answer: Products, customers, consumption, profit outlook, management strength, supply and demand with regard to outputs, and economic data.

   Discussion: Fundamental analysts are concerned with the profitability of a company or industry. Often, the focus will be on hard facts such as earnings, market share, and growth rates. The ultimate objective is to determine whether the market price of the stock or commodity reflects its true value. If the market price is too high, then it would make sense to sell short the investment. If the price in the market is too low relative to the true value of the company or investment, the investor may want to buy the asset or place a bullish options strategy.

4. ____________ analysis is primarily concerned with statistics generated by market activity and the resulting patterns and trends.

   Answer: B—Technical.

Discussion: Technical analysts want to determine if the buying pressure or selling pressure is increasing relative to a specific stock or investment. When buyers are gaining greater control, prices are likely to rise. When sellers seize control, prices will fall. Statistics based on market activity along with patterns or trends can help determine relative levels of buying and selling pressure.

5. Name two common tools of technical analysis.

   Answer: Moving average and momentum indicator.

   Discussion: Moving averages and momentum indicators are among the more commonly used technical indicators, but there are many more.

6. _____________, probably the simplest and most widely used technical tool, calculate price action over a specified period of time as a mean or average.

   Answer: B—Moving averages.

   Discussion: A moving average is the average of a given amount of data plotted on a stock chart using different time frames. For example, a 14-day average of closing prices is calculated by adding the last 14 closes and dividing that number by 14. This simple tool is an easy way to see long-term trends and identify areas of support or resistance.

7. A _____________ utilizes price and volume statistics for predicting the strength or weakness of a current market and any overbought or oversold conditions.

   Answer: C—Momentum indicator.

   Discussion: Momentum trading is the practice of buying or selling an investment based on its price trend. For instance, if a stock has been moving higher on heavy volume for a considerable period of time, it is said to have strong upward momentum. Momentum traders will attempt to profit from this inertia by purchasing that stock during the upward move.

8. _____________ analysis is primarily concerned with the nature and impact of crowd psychology on financial markets.

   Answer: C—Sentiment.

   Discussion: Sentiment analysis gauges investor sentiment by analyzing the group consciousness of the marketplace, using various market criteria that define the market's "state of mind." The goal is to determine if investors, or "the crowd," are bullish or bearish toward the market. When studying market sentiment, the technical analyst generally takes a contrarian approach. That is, if investors are predominantly bullish, the analyst will be bearish (sell stocks). If, on the other hand, the crowd is bearish, the analyst will turn bullish (buy stocks). Examples of indicators used in sentiment analysis include the following: survey of newsletter writers, amount of margin debt, and mutual fund cash levels. The interpretation of these criteria, however, is subjective. Luckily, market analysts do agree that certain measurements strongly suggest a predominantly bullish or bearish tone to the market, but sentiment analysis requires the combination and interpretation of several measurements to reach a conclusion.

9. Name some tools of sentiment analysis.

   Answer: Volatility Index (VIX), VXN, put/call ratios, advisor sentiment, confidence index, odd-lot short sales, mutual fund liquid assets ratio, short interest ratio, over-the-counter (OTC) relative volume, market P/E ratio, and the Dow Jones Industrial Average dividend yield.

   Discussion: A wide variety of sentiment indicators exists for traders to explore. Two of the most popular include the Volatility Index (VIX) and put/call ratios. VIX reflects the implied volatility and premium paid for SPX options and can rise dramatically during periods of uncertainty as investors scramble to hedge portfolios with SPX puts. VIX tends to stay within a range for long periods of months or years. When the VIX either exceeds or drops below this range, a mood of either pessimism (a high VIX) or optimism (a low VIX) prevails.

   Put/call ratios are used as a contrary indicator. Since calls make money when shares or indexes rise, they often represent bullish bets on the part of investors. Conversely, puts increase in value when a stock or index moves lower and, therefore, reflect bearish bets. Again, studying put/call ratios is an exercise in contrary thinking. Specifically, if most market participants (the crowd) are buying puts, it is a sign of negative sentiment and reason to turn bullish. Conversely, a low put/call ratio is interpreted as a market negative since the crowd is excessively bullish, but probably wrong.

10. If you use _____________, you will be trading against the majority view of the marketplace.

    Answer: D—The contrarian approach.

Discussion: Contrarians bet against the crowd. The idea is that the majority of investors can't be correct all of the time. When the majority view becomes too one-sided, it pays to bet against that view. Thus, the contrarian investor does the opposite of what the general consensus may be. Even though this may sound suicidal, time has repeatedly proven this strategy's wisdom.

11. True or False: Fundamental and technical analysis are mutually exclusive—traders should learn to use one or the other.

    Answer: False.

    Discussion: Many successful traders use a combination of technical and fundamental analysis. In general terms, fundamental analysis is the study of the company and technical analysis is the study of the stock price. As a trader, use what works for you.

12. By studying the daily reactions of specific markets to ____________, you can begin to forecast which strategy can be used to make the largest potential profit.

    Answer: D—All of the above (interest rates, seasonal changes, government reports).

    Discussion: Seasonal patterns, economic reports, and changes in interest rates are all factors to consider when studying the day-to-day action in the markets and developing options strategies. Ultimately, these are the factors that can trigger market volatility and end long-term trends.

13. Name three ways you can spot potentially profitable investments when shopping in a retail store.

    Answer:

    1. What products are hot.
    2. Which products have the most store shelf exposure.
    3. Which products a clerk says are literally flying off the shelf.

    Discussion: A simple way to look for investment opportunities is to pay more attention to what is happening in your local area. Visiting retail stores, for example, and understanding what consumers are buying can sometimes help uncover the next great investment.

14. Name four ways to spot potential investments in your everyday life.

    Answer:

    1. When you are driving around, take notice of companies and franchises where you get a good deal as to price, quality, and quantity.
    2. Critique what you already own.
    3. Ask your children what's hot and what's not.
    4. Look around where you work for popular products and services.

    Discussion: The day-to-day trends in your local area often reflect broader trends throughout the economy. A question to ask is, "Who is making money and is there a way for me to profit as well?"

15. Data service providers can relay information in which three ways?

    Answer: Real-time, delayed, and end-of-day.

    Discussion: Many active traders use real-time quote services to trade. However, the cost of real-time quotes can be quite high. Alternatively, traders can use delayed or end-of-day data, which are a bit slower but also less expensive.

16. True or False: If you are going to sit in front of a computer all day long, then you don't really need real-time feeds.

    Answer: False.

    Discussion: Day trading requires real-time quotes. Obviously, end-of-day data will not work because day trading attempts to capture price movements throughout the trading day. Delayed quotes will be too slow. So for those traders who have decided to spend the day in front of the computer, it makes sense to pay extra fees and get real-time data feeds to be as competitive as possible.

17. ______________ was born from the Financial News Network (FNN), which was watched widely by the investment community.

    Answer: B—CNBC.

    Discussion: CNBC, now the most watched financial television news channel, originated from the Financial News Network.

18. The best investments have ______________, which should be monitored over both a short and a long period of time.

    Answer: C—Momentum.

Discussion: Prices move in trends. Momentum is a sign that a trend is healthy and is likely to have staying power. The best investments will therefore have positive momentum. The best shorting opportunities will have downward momentum.

19. An increase in a stock's ______________ signals movement and a good opportunity for investment.

    Answer: B—Volume.

    Discussion: Volume is the engine that makes an investment go. If there is no volume behind an advance or decline, the trend is less likely to have staying power. Rising volume during a stock's advance is a possible sign of an attractive investment opportunity.

20. The best investments have a reasonable ______________ relative to the industry average.

    Answer: C—P/E.

    Discussion: Valuations are an important consideration when looking for stock purchases. A high price-earnings (P/E) ratio is a sign that shares might be overvalued. Therefore, investors will want to ensure that the stock's P/E is reasonable compared to other companies in the industry.

21. Name six ways to spot potential profit-making stock opportunities.

    Answer:

    1. Stocks with greatest percent rise in volume.
    2. Stocks with an increase in price greater than 20 percent.
    3. Stocks with a decrease in price greater than 20 percent.
    4. Stocks with strong (buying)/weak (selling) earnings per share (EPS) growth.
    5. Stocks with strong (buying)/weak (selling) relative strength.
    6. Stocks making new 52-week highs or new 52-week lows.

    Discussion: Technical-oriented traders rely heavily on price and volume data. By studying patterns and relationships, these traders can increase the odds of entering into winning trades. In that respect, the six situations listed have stood the test of time.

22. A low-priced market trades for less than ______________.

    Answer: B—$20.

Discussion: Stocks trading for less than $20 are considered low-priced for options trading purposes.

23. Why is it easier to make money on low-priced markets?

    Answer: D—All of the above (make a high return faster, have less invested to lose, play more stocks with less money).

    Discussion: An investor with a fixed amount of money to invest can generate better returns with low-priced stocks because (1) with lower-priced stocks each dollar move represents a larger percentage move, (2) there is less invested to lose, and (3) you can participate in a greater number of different stocks with the same amount of money.

24. The theory behind ____________, the basis of a mutual fund, is that a larger group of stocks will even out the chances of winning in the long run.

    Answer: C—Both A and B (diversification and a broad portfolio).

    Discussion: A mutual fund is a large pool of money that invests in different types of securities. For example, a stock mutual fund holds a portfolio of stocks. The benefits are that mutual funds allow investors to spread their investments across a broad range of securities and therefore offer diversification.

25. Momentum investors are much more ____________ oriented than mutual fund investors or money managers.

    Answer: A—Short-term.

    Discussion: Momentum investing is an aggressive short-term trading style that is much more active than mutual fund investing. It involves much short-term buying and selling. In most cases, mutual fund investors buy shares and hold those shares over the long term.

26. A long-term indicator of momentum can be measured by looking for a change in price of a stock over the previous ____________.

    Answer: F—Both C and D (60 and 90 days).

    Discussion: Technical analysts look at indicators over different time frames, but 60 and 90 days are common for longer-term momentum indicators.

27. If a stock has increased or decreased in price more than ______________ since yesterday, this can be used to indicate a momentum investment.

    Answer: D—20 percent.

    Discussion: A rule of thumb when looking at daily price moves in a stock is 20 percent. A gain of 20 percent or more suggests strong upward momentum. A decline of 20 percent or greater is a sign of powerful downside momentum.

28. If a stock trades less than ______________ shares daily, try to avoid it in short-term trading.

    Answer: B—300,000.

    Discussion: Illiquid and thinly traded stocks rarely make suitable investments for short-term trading. Traders generally want to focus on stocks that see volume of 300,000 shares or more each day. The greater the volume, the better the stock for trading purposes.

29. To apply the contrarian approach, look at the ______________ list to find stocks that have made major moves down (50 percent or greater) and then look for a rebound.

    Answer: B—Price Percentage Losers.

    Discussion: Use the Price Percentage Losers list to find stocks that have fallen too far, too fast. If a stock is down 50 percent or more, there is a strong chance that it is due to rebound. This would be a contrarian approach because it is betting against the momentum of the stock.

30. The blow-off bottom may have occurred when a stock is coming off a new ______________.

    Answer: C—Low price with high volume.

    Discussion: Blow-off bottoms occur when a stock falls sharply and investors panic. High volume is a sign that a blow-off has occurred. At that time, the stock will come off a low price and begin to move higher.

MEDIA ASSIGNMENT

The purpose of the latest media assignment is to find a source of stock charts and perform some simple analysis. Recall that charts are really windows for viewing the past price patterns of stocks, futures, and indexes. They can provide quick information and, although chart reading is generally considered the domain of technical analysts, almost all investors use charts in one form or another. In addition, with today's online charting capabilities, applying indicators like moving averages is free, quick and simple. In the end, the reader should be able to:

- Access stock charts.
- Create daily, weekly, and monthly charts for stocks like IBM, ExxonMobil, and General Electric.
- Create similar charts for the Dow Jones Industrial Average and the S&P 500.
- Apply moving averages and other indicators.
- Draw trend lines as well as identify support and resistance areas.

VOCABULARY DEFINITIONS

Bar chart: Sometimes called the open-high-low-close (OHLC) chart, it graphs the open, high, low, and settlement prices for a specific trading session over a given period of time.

Blow-off bottom: A sharp and dramatic fall in price accompanied by heavy trading volume. This often occurs when sellers have thrown in the towel and the investment is due to head higher. It is also known as capitulation.

Blow-off top: A steep and rapid increase in price followed by a steep and rapid drop in price. This is an indicator seen in charts and used in technical analysis of stock price and market trends.

Capitulation: When investors en masse have completely given up hope on an investment or market. Capitulation often occurs on heavy, panic-type selling, and is followed by a major advance in the investment or market. It is also known as a blow-off bottom.

Contrarian: An investor who continually bets against the crowd. The contrarian believes that the majority of investors are wrong about the direction of a market or investment at major turning points and that therefore it pays to invest in a manner contrary to popular opinion.

Data feed: An electronic source of information that delivers quotes, news, and other research to a user's computer. Traders rely on data feeds to deliver current prices, news, and charts.

Diversification: Spreading one's assets across a wide variety of investments within a portfolio to minimize the impact of any one security on overall portfolio performance and to reduce the overall risk.

Fund manager: An individual responsible for the day-to-day investment decisions of a mutual fund. Fund managers often receive a performance-based incentive fee for handling the fund.

Fundamental analysis: A type of investment analysis that focuses on company-specific facts from financial statements like the balance sheet and annual reports. Earnings, sales, assets, management, products, and markets are also considered important. This type of analysis is used to determine whether a stock or group of stocks is overvalued or undervalued relative to the current market price.

Momentum: The tendency for the underlying asset to move in trends, higher or lower. As inertia takes hold, sometimes the move can begin to accelerate. When this happens, the asset has strong price momentum.

Moving average: Added to stock charts, these indicators represent average price over time. By averaging prices, the indicator can smooth or eliminate the fluctuations in data and assist in identifying trends.

Moving average convergence/divergence (MACD): Created by Gerald Appel, MACD is a technical chart indicator based on moving averages. It appears on charts as two lines. Crossovers of these two lines generate buy and sell trading signals. Alternatively, some traders plot MACD as a histogram.

Mutual fund: A pooled investment that holds a portfolio of securities. Investors can buy into the pool by purchasing shares. Mutual funds specialize in different types of investments—growth stocks, conservative stocks, bonds, and so on.

On balance volume (OBV): A tool for viewing trends with respect to volume. Developed by Joseph Granville, the indicator measures the buying and selling pressure by looking at daily volume during a stock or market's advance or decline. The math behind the indicator is straightforward. If a stock finishes the day higher, the volume is added to the running total; but if a stock finishes the day lower, the day's volume is subtracted. Traders want to see OBV moving in the same direction (confirming the existing direction).

Price-earnings (P/E) ratio: The price of a stock divided by its annual earnings. Price-to-earnings ratios are often used to determine if a stock is under- or overvalued.

Real-time data: A source of information that is updated live and changes instantaneously as prices change in the marketplace. Real-time data is usually provided for a fee.

Seasonal patterns: A consistent but short-lived rise or drop in market activity that occurs due to predictable changes in climate or calendar.

Sentiment analysis: The study of market psychology. The goal is to determine whether traders and investors are predominantly bullish or bearish toward the stock market. In general, analysts consider excessive amounts of bullish sentiment to indicate short-term market tops. High levels of bearish sentiment often occur near market bottoms.

Technical analysis: A method of evaluating securities by analyzing statistics generated by market activity, such as past prices and volume. Technical analysts do not attempt to measure a security's intrinsic value.

Volume: The amount of trading activity associated with a given security during a period of time. Stock volume is measured in shares, and options volume is based on number of contracts. In addition, volume can be computed over different time frames, such as hours, days, weeks, months, or years.

CHAPTER 18

Tools of the Trade

SUMMARY

This chapter discusses some of the tools available for the stock and options trader, including charts, software programs, seminars, and trading web sites. Option traders need to develop a working knowledge of technical, fundamental, and sentiment analysis, as well as understand how options work. Although studying books can help traders become more knowledgeable, it often takes time and practice to successfully learn the more subtle details of trading.

Although a new trader does not need to learn how to use every tool available, certain tools help flatten the learning curve. For example, the Optionetics web site has a number of free tools, including articles, charts, and option information. Other tools, like Optionetics Platinum, ProfitSource, and Advanced GET from eSignal, might also provide much needed help as you integrate options into your trading approach.

This chapter provides a brief example of how these tools can be used to find explosive trading opportunities. If you are new to the option trading game, then choose a few strategies that you feel will work best for you and learn them inside and out. Too many traders get "analysis paralysis" when they try to use too many tools or technical indicators to find a trade.

QUESTIONS AND EXERCISES

1. True or False: A trader can never use too many tools to make trading decisions.
2. Name some of the tools that are available for the options trader.

   ____

   ____

3. True or False: A new trader should learn and implement every strategy available.
4. Which of the following are chart types used by traders of stocks and options?
   A. Line.
   B. Bar.
   C. Candlestick.
   D. All of the above.
5. Name some of the tools the Optionetics Platinum site can provide for a trader.

   ____

   ____

MEDIA ASSIGNMENT

Take a free tour of the Optionetics web site, as well as the Platinum site. Optionetics.com is free of charge and has an abundance of articles and tools that can be accessed. Although Platinum has a fee, check out the 14-day free trial to access the potentials of this innovative site. By viewing these two sites, a trader can start to work with data that can be systematically gathered and used time and time again to make profits. Many traders have a daily ritual of visiting the Optionetics web site to garner information about the options game from its staff of writers.

VOCABULARY LIST

Bar chart

Candlestick chart

Line chart

Put/call ratio

Volume

SOLUTIONS

1. True or False: A trader can never use too many tools to make trading decisions.

   Answer: False.

   Discussion: Though it is important to have various tools at your disposal, using too many can create confusion. When a trader becomes overwhelmed with analysis tools, he or she may find it hard to decide which factors to follow, and that makes decision making tough.

2. Name some of the tools that are available for the options trader.

   Answer: Internet sites, seminars, software programs, brokers and CNBC.

   Discussion: Some tools are free and some have a cost. Though many traders have become successful without paying for extra services and tools, using these tools can often cut the learning curve down substantially. A carpenter could probably build a house with a hammer and handsaw, but it's a lot easier to use more efficient tools.

3. True or False: A new trader should learn and implement every strategy available.

   Answer: False.

   Discussion: Though a new trader should gain a basic understanding of the various strategies available, it is best to narrow trading choices down to a few strategies. This way a trader can gain specialized knowledge that will create consistent profits rather than trying to be a jack-of-all-trades.

4. Which of the following are chart types used by traders of stocks and options?

   Answer: D—All of the above (line, bar, candlestick).

   Discussion: Traders tend to form their own opinions of what charts work best for them. Though line charts aren't as popular as they once were, there still are traders who choose to use this simple charting tool. Bar charts and candlestick charts are the most popular styles used today because they paint a broader picture of the action of the stock.

5. Name some of the tools the Optionetics Platinum site can provide for a trader.

   Answer: Stock charts, implied volatility charts, historic option data, option search tools, stock search tools and risk graphs.

   Discussion: Though a trader does not need Platinum to become successful, it definitely helps speed up the process. Platinum offers tools that enable traders to search through millions of single option or combination trades in just a matter of seconds. It also provides risk graph analysis of your own personal trades, implied volatility rankings tailored to any option you choose, a trade selection matrix that allows you to match trades with your market preferences, access to easy paper trading through portfolio management with nightly e-mail of profit/loss performance, and historical back-testing capabilities on options going back more than two and a half years.

MEDIA ASSIGNMENT

There are many web sites and books available that will provide information about trading options and stocks. The Optionetics site is one of these and is free, including a discussion board where traders can share ideas and ask questions. By studying the information available on the Optionetics site, you'll become familiar with a variety of tools for your trading arsenal.

Though it requires a fee, the Platinum site is a tool that many options traders say they simply cannot live without. The Platinum web site provides option traders with a variety of powerful tools including:

- End-of-day options price, volume, and open interest data for indexes, stocks, and futures.
- End-of-day options Greeks for all puts and calls.
- Option trade portfolio tracking and profit/loss calculations.
- Implied and historical volatility information and charts.
- Stock ranking tools.
- Option search tools.
- Extensive option analysis tools.
- Complete back-testing of all trades and Platinum functions.

Option trades can be saved online and named along with a text description. Trades can have any combination of stock options and long and short positions. Saved trades can be edited, copied, and sorted. In addition, end-of-day trade performance can be e-mailed each evening to the trader. Option Greeks can be computed for the entire trade as well as each leg, and online trade data can be transferred to other products like Excel.

Platinum offers powerful visual features by allowing the graphical analysis of profit-and-loss risk caused by stock price changes, Greek delta variations, and sensitivity to implied volatility changes. The trade probability of profit and most likely expected profit are also computed on a daily basis.

Some of the key volatility variables and options data that can be plotted include implied volatility (IV), statistical volatility (SV), stock price, volume, put/call ratio, option skew charts, and IV/SV charts for many different time frame combinations.

The stock ranking and option search tools offer the user a high degree of flexibility. Stocks can be ranked using up to 35 different ranking criteria. Many of the rankings are precomputed daily and put online for easy access. These rankings can be saved online in 10 user lists and can be accessed in other Platinum tool sets. The option-searching feature can search a single stock's option chain for option trades as well as traverse multiple stocks in lists simultaneously. Multiple option trading strategies can also be searched using a variety of different search parameters.

Risk graphics of any trade can be computed for different criteria. For back-testing tasks, the web site can operate at any trading date in the past two and a half years. This includes all charts, option tables of data, searches, and risk graphics. In addition, users can enter trades in the past and see how they have evolved to the present. As they enter these trades they have the ability to save them and close them out on their close date.

I encourage those of you new to Platinum to try out the free tour to get a deeper understanding of the software's capabilities. If you are a new user and there is a feature you are confused about, be sure to utilize the context help facility, which is available on virtually every screen in the system. The Platinum site makes it easy to integrate these powerful tools into your own trading.

VOCABULARY DEFINITIONS

Bar chart: A chart that graphs the high, low, and settlement prices for a specific trading session over a given period of time. Also called an OHLC chart.

Candlestick chart: A type of charting that uses a body and shadow for each trading period. Like a bar chart, the open, close, high, and low prices are found in each candlestick.

Line chart: A type of chart that uses only the close of each period. This takes out much of the noise found in the daily movement, but these details are often important to a technical trader.

Put/call ratio: The amount of puts traded on a security compared to the amount of calls. This is a contrarian indicator that helps traders find possible tops and bottoms for a stock or index.

Volume: The amount of shares bought and sold on a stock exchange.

CHAPTER 19

Final Summary

SUMMARY

Traders are constantly bombarded with a multitude of ways to trade stocks and options, leaving many traders unsure of where to start. Optionetics teaches that a systematic approach, used with discipline, can create solid trading profits. Though options traders can benefit from directional strategies, traders can also profit without the need to predict market direction using delta neutral strategies.

In the beginning, new traders need to focus on learning just a couple of the strategies and master them. As your experience increases, along with your success rate, you then can add a wider variety of strategies. Traders need to use proper risk management and money management, allowing limited mistakes to be made. Make sure you use only money that you can afford to lose. In addition, you should not invest all your trading capital at one time.

This chapter provides a trading matrix that can be used to narrow down the appropriate strategies given the level of implied volatility and a trader's view for the stock. Options provide a number of strategies that can be implemented in any type of market environment. However, it is up to the trader to decide what strategies fit the given market scenario.

This chapter also discusses the investing philosophies of some of the most successful investors throughout investing history. Though these investors looked more long-term for their trades, we can learn from their disciplined approaches and viewpoints. Diversification was a common theme, as was having a thorough understanding of the investment. The key to success in trading stocks or options is to take emotion out of the equation.

This may be tough to do; however, by choosing profit and loss exits ahead of time, emotions can be pushed aside when this selling point is reached.

QUESTIONS AND EXERCISES

1. How much time should a new trader take paper trading a new strategy?
   A. None—just jump right in with real money.
   B. One trade.
   C. One week.
   D. At least three months.
2. Using ______________, traders have the opportunity to maximize profits and make consistent returns without the need to predict market direction.
   A. Vertical spreads.
   B. Delta neutral strategies.
   C. Covered writes.
   D. Ratio spreads.
3. Ultimately, only ______________ can take care of your money.
   A. Your broker.
   B. A financial guru.
   C. You.
   D. The IRS.
4. A directional trader has to be right about which of the following assessments?
   A. Direction.
   B. Magnitude of the move.
   C. Time frame of the move.
   D. All of the above.
5. True or False: Understanding volatility is one of the most important components of becoming a successful options trader.
6. Which one of the following strategies would not fit a scenario of low volatility with a bearish bias?
   A. Buy put.
   B. Bear put spread.

C. Buy ITM call.

D. Bull put spread.

7. ______________ is merely another way of expressing a driving need for perfectionism.

A. Fear.

B. Lying to yourself.

C. Greed.

D. Poverty consciousness.

8. Which of the following is/are key for a trader to become successful trading options?

A. A bargain-hunting instinct with the ability to identify undervalued and overvalued options.

B. A sound and well-designed game plan that provides consistent action over time and that prospers in all market conditions.

C. The discipline to follow the game plan.

D. All of the above.

9. What are the three questions every trader should ask before getting into a trade?

1. ____

2. ____

3. ____

MEDIA ASSIGNMENT

By now you should have a good understanding of what is needed to become a successful options trader. Take the time to write down the things you have learned from this book and review these discoveries from time to time. In addition, choose a few strategies that have caught your interest and start paper trading them. If you haven't already done so, start a trading journal to track the details of each trade, as well as to document your thoughts along the way. Hopefully, this book has provided some tangible insights about how to trade options successfully. Now it's up to you to take these ideas and integrate them into your trading plan.

SOLUTIONS

1. How much time should a new trader take paper trading a new strategy?

   Answer: D—At least three months.

   Discussion: Each trader will have his or her own time frame that is needed to paper trade a new strategy. However, most traders should spend at least three months testing a new strategy. A longer amount of time might be necessary if a strong understanding of the strategy is not achieved within three months. Nonetheless, eventually a trader needs to bite the bullet and test these strategies with real money. The key is to start small and build up the amount you trade as your expertise grows.

2. Using ______________, traders have the opportunity to maximize profits and make consistent returns without the need to predict market direction.

   Answer: B—Delta neutral strategies.

   Discussion: Delta neutral strategies help take some of the guesswork out of trading options. Trading directional strategies can be profitable, but the move must be large enough in the predicted direction and within a certain time period. The key to long-term success in the options game is to make consistent returns. It's nice to hit a home run now and then, but the consistent base hitter tends to have the best results all told. Delta neutral trading enables investors to make money regardless of market direction—a revolutionary approach in today's volatile markets.

3. Ultimately, only ______________ can take care of your money.

   Answer: C—You.

   Discussion: Too many traders have found out that listening solely to a broker or financial guru is detrimental to their trading accounts' health. Though we can learn from brokers and various web sites and newsletters, we are the only ones who really care about the success of our trading accounts. It might seem easier to rely on stock and option selections from someone else, but when things go wrong, you need to take responsibility and learn from your mistakes.

4. A directional trader has to be right about which of the following assessments?

   Answer: D—All of the above (direction, magnitude of the move, time frame of the move).

   Discussion: All three of these assessments need to be right in order for a directional trader to see profits. This doesn't mean directional trading can't be profitable, but delta neutral trades are often easier to profit from because they do not need to see a certain market direction. Ultimately, it is the disciplined traders who are successful, regardless of what strategies they implement.

5. True or False: Understanding volatility is one of the most important components of becoming a successful options trader.

   Answer: True.

   Discussion: Too many new traders believe that their experience in the stock market will transfer over to success in trading options. Though it is important to have a basic understanding of the stock market, including technical and fundamental analysis, options do have additional concepts that need to be learned. Mainly, if we do not trade options with the appropriate implied volatility for the given strategy, losses can occur even when our analysis of the underlying stock is correct.

6. Which one of the following strategies would not fit a scenario of low volatility with a bearish bias?

   Answer: D—Bull put spread.

   Discussion: A bull put spread is a credit strategy that is bullish in nature. When volatility is low, we normally want to be the buyer of options. Though the bull put spread uses puts, it is a bullish strategy and does not fit a low-volatility market with a bearish bias. Any trade should be viewed in a risk graph before it is entered to get an idea of what risks there are to the trade and if your expectations will create an appropriate profit.

7. ______________ is merely another way of expressing a driving need for perfectionism.

   Answer: C—Greed.

   Discussion: Perfection has become a driving standard for many people, given the high expectations and competitive nature of today's society. However, perfection is impossible to achieve in the trading game. The successful trader is disciplined and unafraid to take a loss when needed or to take a profit even if it isn't at the apex of the possible gain. Option traders are going to have losses, even when they do everything right. However, it is the disciplined trader who is able to get rid of the emotions of greed and fear who is successful.

8. Which of the following is/are key for a trader to become successful trading options?

   Answer: D—All of the above (a bargain-hunting instinct with the ability to identify undervalued and overvalued options, a sound and well-designed game plan that provides consistent action over time and that prospers in all market conditions, and the discipline to follow the game plan).

Discussion: All three of these elements are key for traders if they want to be successful. As a trader, you need to understand if an option is under- or overvalued in order to enter the best reward/risk trades. You also need to have a plan set up in advance, so that emotion does not hinder your decision making process. Finally, try to develop trading discipline so that you have the courage to stick to your trading plan.

9. What are the three questions every trader should ask before getting into a trade?

   Answer:

   1. What is the market entry?
   2. What is the profit exit?
   3. What is the loss exit?

   Discussion: Before you enter any trade, you should have a set entry point and exit based on profit and loss. Just like an airline flight attendant who tells passengers where the exits are before takeoff, a trader should have a similar plan. Emotion is the major obstacle for both new and experienced traders, and having preset entry and exit points helps alleviate a large amount of emotion-based uncertainty.

FINAL WORD

Regardless of whether you decide to trade stocks, futures, options, or all three, there are certain characteristics that all successful traders possess. These attributes are very important for any trader to acquire if he or she wants to make it in this business over the long haul and continually bring in profits.

The first characteristic and probably the most important is discipline. It is absolutely paramount that a trader has full control of his or her emotional state of mind to be successful at trading. Discipline allows the trader to be more objective and enhances the capacity to identify an opportunity. In addition, it provides the trader with the necessary confidence to refrain from taking action because many times traders feel they must always be involved in the markets. Knowing when to stay out is as important as knowing when to take advantage of an opportunity. This all requires self-control, discipline, and the courage to pull the trigger at the appropriate time.

Next, a good trader needs to be persistent. This means a trader should never take losses personally. Instead a determined trader will attempt to learn from prior mistakes and persist in developing successful trades. This is a fine line, however, because although it is important to learn from mistakes and admit when you are wrong, it is also important to know when not to quit. This type of mentality is also vital when searching for a trading methodology best suited to your style.

Patience is another critical attribute. Many times the trader must wait for the right opportunity versus acting on the wrong ones. Since there are many incorrect actions one can take in the market, it is important to wait for the right opportunities. Many traders are fearful of missing something if they are not always in the market. The patient trader has the confidence to wait for the correct opportunity to present itself.

Another key attribute a good trader must possess is the ability to think independently. Most successful people in any business are independent thinkers. This often requires going against the crowd and establishing a point of view different from the norm. This can be uncomfortable for many people. As a trader, it is important to filter out the opinions of friends, associates, and brokers. Trading strategies and the actual execution of trades involve a singleness of purpose and firm resolve. That is why it is so essential for a good trader to develop independent thinking and avoid the herd mentality.

Contrary thinking is also an important characteristic. People have a hard time going against the crowd. Cultivating the art of contrary thinking allows the trader to take actions that oppose the majority. This is important because (generally) the majority is wrong and public losses are commonplace. So it is essential to be able to evaluate what the crowd is thinking and have the courage to take an independent approach to the market. Contrary opinion will also help the trader avoid being trapped when panic takes hold of a market. In this way, a good trader will be able to take advantage of the emotional extremes in the market and profit from them.

Good traders must also be truthful with themselves and accurately assess their strengths and weaknesses. This is rarely easy and is sporadically done by most traders. However, recognizing the truth is a key requirement for achieving success as a trader. A good trader must continually engage in a process of self-reflection. Learning to take an honest inventory of your own motivations, priorities, and actions will enable you to accentuate your strengths and work on the weaknesses that make you vulnerable in the market.

A dedicated trader must be able to act quickly and flawlessly execute his or her trading plan. There is a clear and important distinction between developing a sense of urgency and acting impulsively. A good trader wants to constantly pay attention and be poised to take action without being too spontaneous or whimsical. The market can move very fast at times, so it is important not to get overwhelmed by indecision and fear. Otherwise the trader gets a sense of paralysis and no action will be taken. It is not enough to be in the right place at the right time; you must also be able to take correct action.

These key attributes have to be part of a trader's skill set for the trader to be successful over the long term. I encourage you to review the preceding paragraphs as your trading career progresses. Continually trying to improve in all these areas is a lifelong commitment. Your efforts are sure to be well rewarded in the form of future trading profits.

Good luck and great trading!

GEORGE A. FONTANILLS
Miami Beach, Florida
December 2004